PLAYS FOR PERFORMANCE

*A series designed for
contemporary production and study
Edited by
Nicholas Rudall and Bernard Sahlins*

GEORGES FEYDEAU

Paradise Hotel

In a New Translation by
Nicholas Rudall

Ivan R. Dee
CHICAGO

Library of Congress Cataloging-in-Publication Data:
Feydeau, Georges, 1862–1921.
    [Hôtel du libre-échange. English]
    Paradise hotel / Georges Feydeau ; in a new translation by Nicholas Rudall.
        p.   cm. — (Plays for performance)
    Translation of: L'Hôtel du libre-échange.
    ISBN 0-929587-48-0 (cloth : acid-free paper)
    ISBN 0-929587-45-6 (pbk. : acid-free paper)
    I. Rudall, Nicholas. II. Title. III. Series.
PQ2611.E86H613   1990
842'.8—dc20
                                                            90-39774

INTRODUCTION

To perform Feydeau well the actors and their directors need a deeper sense of the real than an aspiration to some theoretical farcical style. The death of farce is the distorted face, the bulging eyes, the contorted body of the actor trying to be funny. Farce is funny for the audience only when it is deadly serious for the characters in the play. For them there is only the pursuit of the unattainable and the fear of discovery. Sexual infidelity, the stuff of Feydeau farce, is in real life not pretty. Nor is it pretty for Feydeau's characters.

The Set

Feydeau has provided a lengthy set of stage directions which certainly describe his own proscenium arch productions. Here is a description of what is needed in each act.

Act 1. A room in Pinglet's house that serves as a living room (a couch, a chair perhaps) and as his work room. He is a contractor. His desk needs architectural plans, protractors, pencils, set squares, etc. It should be out of the way, perhaps up-stage in front of the necessary bay window. There are bookshelves, but they are not used. There are three doors, one leading to Madame Pinglet's quarters, one leading to the bedroom, and the entrance to the apartment with a (not necessarily visible) hallway leading to a neighbor's apartment.

3

There is a table by the doorway with a telephone and a telephone directory. There is a bolt on the outside and inside of the door, strange as that may seem. There is a coffee table. There is coffee (or tea) in a pot on the tray. The windows must work, since at the end of the act Pinglet must climb out of them, down a rope ladder that serves as a fire escape. The windows should therefore suggest that this apartment is on the second floor. The escape ladder could be in a box or be rolled up and attached to the underside of the sill. There could be a balcony outside the window to make the exit easier. Feydeau suggests a view of the Eiffel tower. The window could also show that it is raining.

Act 2. The Paradise Hotel. There are a number of very tricky requirements. Scenes take place in a number of different areas, different rooms. As the lights go off in one area they come on in another. The place is seedy. This translation suggests that the manager is "Eastern," perhaps Indian, whether in truth or by design. He certainly fractures his clichés. The hotel could well benefit from some late Victorian Eastern *kitsch*. The lobby must have a desk with keys, and a cleaver. There must be a drawer containing a hand drill. From the lobby there is direct access to the entrance to the hotel (there is a front doorbell). But the front door, while visible to the characters in the lobby, is not visible to the audience. On one side is the room to be occupied by M. Pinglet and M. Paillardin. It must have an entrance door off the lobby and it must have a door into the bathroom. It contains a working fireplace. Pinglet must be pushed from the entrance door into the fireplace. In a few seconds his face must be blackened with "soot." There is a "fake" chair which must collapse when

4

Pinglet sits on it. There is a table with room for a tray for a teapot, mug, and seven cups and saucers. An ashtray. There must be room for six chairs which have to be brought in very quickly from the lobby or from the front hallway. Pinglet at one point sits on the table with his back to the wall that attaches to the lobby. The drill must give the appearance of piercing that wall and sticking Pinglet.

The other main room is for Paillardin and Mathieu and his daughters. It needs a bed with movable curtains, large enough to conceal two people. It needs space for four cots. There is a table with space for a box of cigars, a small suitcase, and a set of hairbrushes. There are *two* doors in the room—separate bathrooms. In the original play, the girls light spirit (kerosene) "curler warmers" for their hair. It is simpler and just as effective for them to light candle "night lights" as the ghosts. Elsewhere on stage, probably on an upper level, there is a doorway to Chervet's room and an exit for Pinglet to go to be sick.

Act 3. The most difficult aspect of Act 3 is the following: Pinglet must return with his face covered in soot. It must be removed *very* quickly, theoretically with a towel or napkin that M. Paillardin dips in a glass of water (which must be brought on by the maid at the end of Act 1). That napkin (theoretically) is put over the face of Maxime as a means of hiding himself. The soot is (theoretically) transferred to his face. Napkins need to be switched, soot needs to be easily put on in Act 2, easily removed in Act 3. We used powder in Act 2; the actor switched to grease paint at intermission and wiped it off in Act 3. Finally there is the unanswerable question of the lock and key. In Act 1 Madame Pinglet leaves with the key to the en-

5

trance door but clearly must also bolt it from the outside, for Pinglet doesn't even look for his own key. When he returns in Act 3, he accidentally finds his key in his bathrobe pocket. And clearly he needs the bolt on the outside to be intact in order to secure his alibi.

The Translation

This is a complete translation with some important adaptations. The title was chosen because one popular early version of the play was *Hotel Paradisio*. It also provided an ironic commentary on the seediness of the locale. The original title translated as *The Free Trade Hotel,* or some such. Some scenes were just too long or simply did not have a contemporary comic equivalent. They were pruned or cut. For example, the scene between Victoire and Maxime in Act 1 was interminable. A lengthy interchange about the different types of limestone to be found in Paris has been cut altogether. The stuttering of Pinglet is racier in potential in this version and therefore ultimately more innocent. But in reality very little has been changed.

A note to the actors: when a character has a number of repetitions in his diction, do not give more weight to one word or phrase than another. I have used repetition to achieve a Gallicism of style. For example, "It's true. It's true," if repeated rapidly with no distinction of emphasis can become the English equivalent of the very French "C'est vrai, n'est ce pas?"

Bon chance.

This translation was first performed on November 10, 1989, at the Court Theatre at the University of Chicago, with the following cast:

BENOIT PINGLET	Nicholas Rudall
ANGELIQUE PINGLET	Denise du Maurier
DRESSMAKER	Jerry Rooney
MARCELLE PAILLARDIN	Linda Emond
HENRI PAILLARDIN	Gerry Becker
MAXIME	Ray Chapman
VICTOIRE	Joan Elizabeth
MATHIEU	Peter Siragusa
PORTERS	Brian-Mark Conover, Jerry Rooney, Kevin McCoy, Edward Torres

Mathieu's daughters:

VIOLET	Holly Maples
MARGARITE	Monica Dionne Dyson
PERVENCHE	Paula Jane Wilson
PAQUERETTE	Flora Diaz
BASTIEN	Victor D'Altorio
BOULOT	Kevin McCoy
CHERVET	Jerry Rooney
ANTOINETTE	Patrice Fletcher
ERNEST	Brian-Mark Conover
INSPECTOR BOUCARD	Jerry Rooney
POLICEMEN	Brian-Mark Conover, Edward Torres

Directed by Kyle Donnelly
Scenic Design by Jeff Bauer
Lighting Design by Rita Pietraszek
Costume Design by Claudia Boddy

Paradise Hotel

ACT 1

PINGLET: *(singing as he works)* Oh come, oh come, my sweetness and my light. A voice like angels in the night.

ANGELIQUE: *(offstage)* Pinglet!

PINGLET: *(aside)* Angelique—my little peach.

(she enters with two samples of material)

ANGELIQUE: My dressmaker is here.

PINGLET: Oh, my God! What do you want me to do about it?

ANGELIQUE: Stop working when I'm talking to you!

PINGLET: Voice like a buzz saw! My little Apricot—I'm working very hard on the house that I'm building with Paillardin.

ANGELIQUE: It can wait.

PINGLET: Yes, my plum.

ANGELIQUE: I don't know which fabric to choose. ...What do you think?

PINGLET: Is it for the couch?

ANGELIQUE: No, you idiot! It's for a dress for me.

PINGLET: I rather like that one.

ANGELIQUE: Good. Very good. Then I'll take this one.

PINGLET: What was the point of asking ...?

ANGELIQUE: Because I know you have no taste.... I wouldn't be caught dead in that other one.

PINGLET: Nice—yes. Very nice. Isn't she a peach?

ANGELIQUE: Get on with it! *(exits)*

PINGLET: Yes, my plum. Yeeeech! That's not a wife—it's Attila the Hun! And I married for love! God Almighty! We eloped! Ha! It's twenty years ago, of course. You know, if we could only see what they'd be like twenty years on we wouldn't marry them twenty years back.... *(at the window)* It's pouring. I'd never let my son get married.... Haven't got a son—never will. Just the thought of ... No no no no no no no. *(a knock at the door)* Come in! *(Marcelle enters carrying a handkerchief)* ... Ah, Madame Paillardin! Yes yes yes yes yes yes.

MARCELLE: *(moody)* Good morning, my dear Pinglet. Should you be receiving me in your dressing gown?

PINGLET: One of the perks of living next door. We can come and go as we please.

MARCELLE: Yes, it's such a comfort. Is your wife in?

PINGLET: Yes, she's negotiating total surrender with her dressmaker. How's your husband?

MARCELLE: How should I know?

PINGLET: *(holding her hands and looking into her eyes)* What's the matter?

MARCELLE: Nothing.

PINGLET: Your eyes are all red! What's the—

MARCELLE: Oh, nothing, nothing.... It's always the same thing.... We've quarreled again.

12

PINGLET: Oh, you poor little thing. Has he been hard on you?

MARCELLE: No, ah ha! No. If he was there'd be some hope. I think he'd find an old shoe more attractive. But.... Let's not talk about it. It upsets me terribly.... I'm going to look for your wife.

PINGLET: You know what? I think I'll give your husband a piece of my mind ... chew him out a bit.

MARCELLE: Oh, no no no. Please don't ... don't breathe a word.... I mean, what good do you think it would do? It'll have no effect ... you might as well ask a one-armed man to play the fiddle. *(exits)*

PINGLET: Oh, what a woman!! Oooaahh, ooh la la.... My wife is always telling me that I'm finished, washed up.... Weeell, if she means finished with her, she's right. But with Madame Paillardin.... Oohh, just give me a chance.... Finished! Just push the old Go button. But ... there it is ... she's married ... married to a frozen halibut. I can call him that. He's my best friend. If you can't call your best friend a frozen halibut, who can ... you call—well, I wish he wasn't my best friend. If only I was absolutely sure that I could seduce her. But there it is ... I'm *not* absolutely sure I could seduce ... And it would be stupid to try, and all I'd get is a punch in the mouth ... basically ... from my best friend.

(he begins to unroll a plan)

Now what does the frozen halibut have for me here? He's out of his mind! Look at this ... limestone! For the supporting wall! Architects! They know nothing about engineering. Nothing! Theory, that's all. We spend half our time covering their assumptions. Limestone! Fish brain! Still, his wife's gorgeous....

(Paillardin enters)

PAILLARDIN: Morning, Pinglet. Hope I'm not disturbing you?

PINGLET: Not at all.... What the goddamn hell do you think your playing at?

PAILLARDIN: What?

PINGLET: You want to use limestone for a supporting wall? Fish brain....

PAILLARDIN: What supporting wall? What do you expect me to use?

PINGLET: Use your head! Anything that's hard.

PAILLARDIN: *(bored)* Use what you like.... I don't care. Is my wife here?

PINGLET: In there. With mine. What have you been doing to her, Paillardin?

PAILLARDIN: Why do you ask ... has she been complaining?

PINGLET: She never complains. You've only got to look at her.

PAILLARDIN: She's impossible.... I don't know what more I can do. I give her everything.... I don't cheat on her.... I don't have a mistress.

PINGLET: You don't have a mistress.... What kind of a husband are you?! Do your duty.

PAILLARDIN: I do. But it's not enough. She says I'm not ... affectionate enough.

PINGLET: Well? Aren't you?

14

PAILLARDIN: I mean, if you've got to be affectionate to your wife, what are things coming to? Are you "affectionate" with yours?

PINGLET: Have you looked at her recently? Twenty years in the bottle.

PAILLARDIN: Not a bad vintage!

PINGLET: Not bad for wine ... but with mine the cork's stuck.

PAILLARDIN: Wish I could say that about us. Marcelle and I have been married five years and she still thinks all that hanky-panky is important. I mean, if you get married just to go to bed with some-one, you might as well take a mistress.

PINGLET: What a fine moral sense.

PAILLARDIN: No, listen ... I mean ... I work hard ... all day. All day I'm at the drawing board.... I come home ... exhausted. I go to bed—I go to sleep. My wife doesn't understand that ... can't accept it. Says I don't understand her needs.

PINGLET: Well? Maybe she has a point.

PAILLARDIN: I never actually liked doing it in the first place. Ever. I suppose that's why I got married. Not my sort of thing really.

PINGLET: Amazing.... You're what we call an iceberg.

PAILLARDIN: And you? You're so hot?

PINGLET: You don't know me, my friend.... Inside here—lava ... magma ... bubbling, throbbing ... but with no place to erupt....

PAILLARDIN: Don't make me laugh! You! A volcano!

PINGLET: More than you, in any case....

15

PAILLARDIN: What do you mean?

PINGLET: Well, you! You've got no lava in you at all!

PAILLARDIN: No?

PINGLET: A volcano without lava is no volcano. It's just a mountain with a boring little hole on top.

PAILLARDIN: Oh, that reminds me.... Could I borrow your maid?

PINGLET: My maid! What do you want her for?

PAILLARDIN: Not for me, you fool.... For my nephew ... Maxime.

PINGLET: That makes it respectable?

PAILLARDIN: Why can't you take anything seriously? Poor kid! Now there's someone who doesn't think about all that hanky-panky. He's a bookworm. Nothing on his mind but philosophy.

PINGLET: Philosophy? At his age? What's he going to do when he gets old?

PAILLARDIN: The point is ... he's starting his first term at the Lycee ... to study philosophy. And I haven't got a servant to take him there—I gave mine the sack, remember? And he must have a servant ... to keep up appearances. ...

PINGLET: Why don't you go with him yourself?

PAILLARDIN: Haven't got time. My day is completely booked up ... and tonight I have to sleep in town.

PINGLET: Ah ha. The tip of the iceberg.

PAILLARDIN: Alone!

PINGLET: I don't believe you.

PAILLARDIN: Yes, well, it's true. I have to spend the night in some awful little hotel. They claim it's haunted.... Poltergeists! Ghosts that moan in the night.

PINGLET: I thought you didn't have that problem.

PAILLARDIN: What? Yes. Well. Ghosts that go bump in the night.... If I see one face to face—I still won't believe it. No, I've made up my mind.... I know what's making the noise ... the drains!

PINGLET: Of course.

PAILLARDIN: The manager of the hotel wants to break his lease. The owner wants to sue him ... and the court is calling me in as an "expert witness." So I have to sleep there overnight. And in the morning I shall pass ... judgment.

PINGLET: Flatulence ... probably ... in the drains.

PAILLARDIN: Precisely. *(leaving)*

PINGLET: Wait a minute. What about your wife? Won't you make up with her first?

PAILLARDIN: How can I? She's been making scene after scene all day. She says I do everything I can to leave her by herself. She has to understand that I'm an architect first and a husband second.

PINGLET: Take care, my friend. Somebody else may come first if you don't watch out.

PAILLARDIN: What do you mean?

PINGLET: I don't want to give you advice ... but ... you're playing a dangerous game. Women are—and your wife in particular—women are passionate creatures. And God forbid ... if ever your wife were to cheat on you ... it'd be your own fault.

PAILLARDIN: My wife cheat on me! Ha! In the first place, where would she find a lover? I mean, *(snapping his fingers)* just like that! That only happens in the theatre.

PINGLET: Yes, well. Good. Off you go!

PAILLARDIN: I'm going.

PINGLET: No, you're right Paillardin. . . . If ever your wife cheats on you, I'll fall over backwards. *(aside)* Preferably with her on top!

(knock on door)

PINGLET: Come in!

PAILLARDIN: Oh, it's you Maxime.

(Maxime enters with a book in hand)

MAXIME: Yes ... Uncle ... Monsieur Pinglet, I'm terribly sorry to disturb you.

PINGLET: You're not.

PAILLARDIN: What do you want?

(Maxime searches the room for his book)

MAXIME: I wanted to ask you, Monsieur Pinglet—I must have left it here. Have you found it? I can't find my book?

PINGLET: What book?

MAXIME: Kant.

PINGLET: Can't what?

MAXIME: Just Kant.

PINGLET: I know you can't, but what can't you find?

MAXIME: Kant's *Moral Philosophy*. I'm comparing it to Descartes.

PAILLARDIN: Oh, *The Treatise on the Passions*.

MAXIME: Yes.

PINGLET: It's a manual?

PAILLARDIN AND MAXIME: Yes, Immanuel Kant.

PINGLET: *(suggestively)* A handbook?

PAILLARDIN: Pinglet!

PINGLET: Just a question. It's a treatise. A handbook. A manual....

(Victoire enters)

VICTOIRE: Sir!

PINGLET: What?

VICTOIRE: Madame wants you.

PINGLET: Now? Oh. Why?

VICTOIRE: She's with the dressmaker, sir. She needs your "good taste."

PINGLET: Good taste? She always chooses the opposite of what I pick. Anyway... I'm going.

PAILLARDIN: Maxime! *(who is rummaging in the drawers)* What are you doing?

MAXIME: Uncle. I'm looking for my book!

PINGLET: No, no. It's not here! Leave my drawers alone! Victoire, he's lost his book. A manual.

(Victoire finds the book)

MAXIME: Immanuel Kant!

PINGLET: Never mind. Victoire, will you go to the Lycee this evening with Monsieur Maxime?

VICTOIRE: Me, monsieur? My pleasure.

PINGLET: I'm not talking about pleasure. I want you to take him to school. *(to Maxime)* At what time?

MAXIME: By nine, Monsieur Pinglet.

VICTOIRE: Yes, sir.

PAILLARDIN: *(to Pinglet)* Thanks, Pinglet, you know?

PINGLET: It's nothing.

(Maxime reads)

MADAME PINGLET: *(offstage)* Pinglet!

PINGLET: There she blows! Coming, my peach! What a voice. Come on Paillardin—you want to see my wife trying her dress on? *(pushing him)* Then go ahead.

MADAME PINGLET: *Pinglet?*

PINGLET: Maybe she's discovered oil. *(they exit)*

MAXIME: Where was I? Ah ... "Passion in an emotion of the soul aroused by the impulses of man's animal nature which make him couple with objects that seem suitable...."

VICTOIRE: What's the book, Monsieur Maxime?

MAXIME: This? *Treatise on Passion.*

VICTOIRE: So what are you doing, exactly?

MAXIME: Studying passion.

VICTOIRE: In that position? *(She flirts ... Maxime ignores her. Victoire moves behind him.)* Can I give you a hand? *(she sits)*

MAXIME: How can I study passion with a woman sitting next to me? *(he moves)*

VICTOIRE: I might be able to suggest a thing or two.

MAXIME: You've read Descartes?

VICTOIRE: Hasn't everybody?

MAXIME: What else do you read?

VICTOIRE: Palms.

MAXIME: Oh. *(he returns to his reading)*

VICTOIRE: He's a nice-looking boy, rugged almost. Monsieur Maxime, have you ever been a naughty little boy? *(she sits closer to him, takes his hand, etc.)*

MAXIME: "There is a distinction to be made between idealistic love and sensual love. The passion a man feels for his mistress is different from the feeling a father has for his children. We can separate, philosophically, love and lust. . . ." What did you say?

VICTOIRE: I said, have you ever been a naughty little boy?

(she puts his hand on her knee)

MAXIME: "Nevertheless they are similar inasmuch as they are both ... passions."

VICTOIRE: What are you doing with your hand?

MAXIME: "The love the father has for his children..."

VICTOIRE: Taking advantage of a girl in my position! Putting your warm little hand where you shouldn't ... !

MAXIME: I didn't put my hand anywhere.

VICTOIRE: You put it on my knee! Dirty little devil. *(she puts it on her knee)* I bet that's all you think about. Putting your hands on girls' knees.

MAXIME: All I'm trying to do is read a book. Philosophy. *(she slides his hand up her leg)*

VICTOIRE: Philosophy. Is that what they call it nowadays?

MAXIME: Look, Victoire, I am trying to study passion.... How can I do that if you keep interrupting me?

VICTOIRE: I could understand a little squeeze, a squeeze I could understand.... But putting it there and keeping it there *(she puts his hand on her breast)*. Your hot little hand. Take it off. I'm going to have to tell your uncle. I really am.

MAXIME: Tell him what?

VICTOIRE: Don't give me that! "Tell him what," Monsieur Innocent! Take your hand off! Right now! Or I'll scream. I'll scream so loud.... *(she puts his hand on her breast)*

MAXIME: Please. No. Please don't scream!

VICTOIRE: Just try to stop me. *(sotto voce)* Help.

MAXIME: How?

VICTOIRE: Cover my mouth. Help. Help.

MAXIME: I can't. Look! *(he has the book in one hand and she has placed his other over her breast)*

VICTOIRE: Put your mouth firmly on mine, Monsieur ... otherwise I'll scream so loud the whole family will be in here like a shot. *(gets on top, forces him, etc.)* Stop! You brute! You savage! *(she kisses him, etc.)*

MAXIME: *(he emerges)* What a curious sensation.... Not altogether unpleasant.

VICTOIRE: Don't you ever try that again! Or you'll

be in serious trouble.... I've got to get back to work.... I'll take you to school later. *(exits)*

MAXIME: "The affection that people in love feel for one another..."

(Marcelle, Paillardin, Angelique, and Pinglet enter)

MARCELLE: Oh, oh. I've had enough.

PAILLARDIN: Once and for all.... What is the matter with you, woman?

MARCELLE: You make life impossible.

ANGELIQUE: My dear, wait till you've been married twenty years.

PINGLET: What are you complaining about? ... I've made you happy.

PAILLARDIN: *(to Marcelle)* So have I.

ANGELIQUE AND MARCELLE: Happy? You've made me happy?

PAILLARDIN AND PINGLET: Yes, I have.

ANGELIQUE AND MARCELLE: No, you haven't.

PAILLARDIN AND PINGLET: Yes, we have.

ANGELIQUE AND MARCELLE: No, you haven't.

MAXIME: *(leaving)* I'm going to the zoo, it's more peaceful.

MARCELLE: What I ask myself is ... why, why, why am I married ... to this ... thing. What do I get out of it?... nothing. He's not a husband, he's a dead fish.

PAILLARDIN: Oh, in public!

MARCELLE: All I do is keep house. That's what he married me for. That's all. He married me to

23

wash his socks and fold his shorts. I'm nothing to him. I might as well not be there—he never touches me.

ANGELIQUE: What! Poor dear.... He never ... tou— is that true? *(to Paillardin)* That's disgusting.

PAILLARDIN: It's not true. Not true. She's exaggerating.

ANGELIQUE: *(to Paillardin)* Pinglet and I have been married for twenty years, but he has never stopped ... well, he's never behaved like that.

PAILLARDIN: *(to Pinglet)* Is that true?

PINGLET: She's exaggerating.

PAILLARDIN: Well ... what is it you want? I suppose you want me to give up this consulting job tonight? Is that it?

MARCELLE: Go ... go ... play with your drains ... I don't care ... look ... if you're here or if you're there, we're just as far apart.

PAILLARDIN: She never stops.

MARCELLE: I tell you here and now, in front of everybody, that I'm going to start looking around.... It is impossible to be an honest woman and a faithful wife in this marriage.

PAILLARDIN: Fine. Good. Good. Start looking around.

PINGLET: She has a point.

PAILLARDIN: Don't stick your ... your ... whatchamacallit in this. Keep your whatchamacallit out of this.

MARCELLE: Be careful. That's all I'm saying. One day I might start looking around, and I just might find the happiness I never get at home.

PAILLARDIN: You, ha! Never.

MARCELLE: Why not? There are lots of women ... lots ... and much plainer than me, who have found lovers.

PAILLARDIN: Then what are you waiting for? Do you think I'd care? Go ahead ... take a lover.

MARCELLE: Don't tempt me.... If I wanted to... I know ... I know lots of men.

PAILLARDIN: Then go and find them. Find yourself a *man*.

ANGELIQUE: Paillardin, you've gone far enough.

PAILLARDIN: Me? She's gone far enough. Let her go.... Let her find her lover boy. All I ask is that when she finds him ... he keeps her.

MARCELLE: Monsieur Pinglet, listen to him, listen to him.

PINGLET: It's crazy, you're crazy, he's crazy.

MARCELLE: I think you're right. Well ... you will get what you asked for.

PAILLARDIN: Wonderful. *(exiting)* Good evening.

ANGELIQUE: Paillardin, look ... kiss and make up.

PAILLARDIN: Me? Never, never, never, never.

ANGELIQUE: Paillardin! Paillardin! *(She follows him out. Pinglet runs after them.)*

PINGLET: You're making a big mistake ... a big— *(turns back into room)* a very big mistake....

MARCELLE: You heard what he said? You heard what my husband said to me? Oh nice, very nice.

PINGLET: Marcelle, Marcelle I love you.

MARCELLE: What?

PINGLET: *(slapping his own wrist)* Wrong. He's crazy.... Didn't I tell him? You're crazy, I said. You're making a big mistake, I said ... I did my duty ... as his best friend.

MARCELLE: Yes. What? I ... I ... yes, you did!

PINGLET: You're making a big mistake, I said. But he didn't care.... I mean, he told you to "go ahead" when you threatened ... to take a lover. Well, in my opinion ... as a good wife ... you should do as you're told and take a lover.

MARCELLE: I ... I ... think you're right.

PINGLET: And it's not as though there's no one around! I ... Marcelle, I am here.

MARCELLE: You?

PINGLET: Yes, me. I only know one thing. He insulted you in my presence. I cannot permit that. He challenged you to find a lover. I accept that challenge. I shall be your lover.

MARCELLE: You?

PINGLET: Yes. I have a duty to my best friend. He laid down the gauntlet. I shall pick it up. Chivalry is not dead. Marcelle ... Marcelle ... I love you. *(he kneels and takes her hand)*

MARCELLE: Wait. Wait. Wait. Wait. Monsieur Pinglet ... think a moment. My duty to my husband!

PINGLET: Poor little wounded creature. She talks of her duty to her husband. Ah, Marcelle, there are times in this life when we must make the ultimate sacrifice and forget our duty to our husbands.

26

MARCELLE: Oh?!

PINGLET: And what about me? And Madame Pinglet? Don't you think it hurts my sense of duty to her? But ... nothing can hold me back. Into the breach, so to speak. There is a higher duty.

MARCELLE: Yes!

PINGLET: We have been insulted. You and I. Into the breach.

MARCELLE: Yes!

PINGLET: Into the breach.

MARCELLE: Why do you keep saying that?

PINGLET: Together! *(he embraces her)*

MARCELLE: Pinglet, no. I can't.

PINGLET: What! You're afraid? Ah, Marcelle. Have you already forgotten how he humiliated you? In front of everybody?

MARCELLE: I shall never forget.

PINGLET: You talk of *your* duty. Ha! Duty. Does he think of his!?

MARCELLE: That's true.

PINGLET: So ... do you have to think of yours?!

MARCELLE: No. I don't.

PINGLET: To think that he has the most beautiful dream-wife in the world and he never touches her—all he thinks of is ... drains.

MARCELLE: You're right. *(she cries) (he wipes her eyes with her handkerchief)* That's mine!

PINGLET: He doesn't love you. He's not a ... a ...

27

lover.... So, vengeance! Ah, bubbling, throbbing vengeance!

MARCELLE: You're right. Oh, thank you, thank you for showing me my duty.

PINGLET: You'll get to know what sort of man I am. Tender, loving ... all, all yours.

MARCELLE: Ah, Pinglet. It's a pity you're so unattractive, but you do know the way to a woman's heart.

PINGLET: Thank you, Marcelle. Thank you.

MARCELLE: God knows if you'd tried this half an hour ago, I'd have been physically ill.

PINGLET: Yes, but I picked the right opening, so to speak, the moment to leap into the breach.

MARCELLE: So now, I say to you: ... Speak, Pinglet. Your word is my command.

PINGLET: *(taking her in his arms)* Oh, Marcelle, Marcelle. You are taking me to the land of my dreams, sweet ecstatic dreams.

ANGELIQUE: *(offstage)* Pinglet!

PINGLET: There goes the alarm clock. Marcelle, there's no time to lose. Your husband won't be at home tonight. You're free. And I'll see to it that I'll be free as well.

MARCELLE: Yes?

PINGLET: I'll come to get you and we'll go ...

MARCELLE: Where?

PINGLET: I don't know yet. But ... I'll find somewhere. I'll let you know. And then, vengeance will be ours, saith Pinglet! Here it comes. Take cover.

ANGELIQUE: *(enters)* Ah, there you are, Pinglet. You really know how to pick your friends, don't you? The impudence!

PINGLET: What do you mean?

ANGELIQUE: I was only trying to patch things up— out of the kindness of my heart, just thinking of you, Marcelle, and do you know what he said— "Keep your fat face out of other people's business." Well!

MARCELLE: That doesn't surprise me.

PINGLET: How rude! *(aside)* She's not that fat.

ANGELIQUE: What?

PINGLET: He said that?

ANGELIQUE: Yes!

PINGLET: To an older woman?

ANGELIQUE: That's not the point. *(to Marcelle)* Oh, Marcelle, I feel so sorry for you.... To have a husband like that!

MARCELLE: Well ... he's going to get it.

ANGELIQUE: What do you mean?

MARCELLE: Nothing.

ANGELIQUE: If Pinglet ever behaved like that ...

MARCELLE: What would you do?

ANGELIQUE: I'd take a lover.

PINGLET: Angelique! You wouldn't!...

ANGELIQUE: Just try me.

PINGLET: I'd love to watch! Death by asphyxiation.

VICTOIRE: *(enters with letters on a salver)* The mail, madam. And a dress has arrived next door for Madame Paillardin.

MARCELLE: Just a little thing I've had made.... Excuse me!

ANGELIQUE: Off you go. There's nothing like a new dress when the marriage bed gets bumpy. Bye bye, my dear.

MARCELLE: Bye bye. *(to Pinglet)* And bye bye to you.

PINGLET: Bye bye. We're all settled? *(to her)* Yes?

MARCELLE: Yes. He's been asking for it. *(exits)*

PINGLET: And I'm going to get it.

VICTOIRE: The mail, madame.

ANGELIQUE: Thank you. Put it down.

PINGLET: Now. Let's think.... Where? A little love nest ... discreet ... romantic. What a dummy! Of course, the directory. *(he looks for the telephone directory)*

ANGELIQUE: Don't make so much noise! ... Victoire, I won't be dining at home this evening.

PINGLET: What luck! *(to her)* You won't, my peach? Er ... where will you ...

ANGELIQUE: At my sister's on the Ville D'Avray. She's not getting any better.... Look, *(giving him the letter)* if I don't get back tonight, don't worry.... I'll spend the night there if she needs me.

PINGLET: Oh! Great! Great!

ANGELIQUE: What?

PINGLET: Don't be late!

ANGELIQUE: So ... dinner for one this evening, Victoire.

VICTOIRE: Yes, ma'am.

PINGLET: Hotels ... hotels ... *(picking up the telephone directory)* Hotels. Let's see.

ANGELIQUE: Ah ... my dressmaker's sent his bill.

PINGLET: I've got it!

ANGELIQUE: Got what?

PINGLET: Nothing ... I said ... you got it ... your dressmaker's bill.

ANGELIQUE: I know ... I just told you.

PINGLET: Ah, yes.

ANGELIQUE: Sometimes. Pinglet, sometimes you say the stupidest things.

PINGLET: *(aside)* Yes, my little grapefruit. Yes. Now ... Hotel Hotspot.... Not really.... The Tomcat Hotel. Good God no.

ANGELIQUE: *(reading another letter)* Oh!

PINGLET: What?

ANGELIQUE: The idea! Sending such things to a respectable woman.

PINGLET: What is it?

ANGELIQUE: Fliers, for a hotel. Three of them.

PINGLET: A hotel?

ANGELIQUE: Listen to this, "The Paradise Hotel, 220 rue de Provence. Privacy and discretion our motto. Catering to married couples—together or separate."

31

PINGLET: Together or ... separate. It says that?

ANGELIQUE: Yes, look.

PINGLET: So it does.

ANGELIQUE: It's a hotel for hanky-panky, if you ask me.

PINGLET: Obviously. *(aside)* "Hanky-panky, hanky-panky." Rooms at all prices.

ANGELIQUE: "Group rates available!"

PINGLET: Disgusting. Group rates!

ANGELIQUE: I can't imagine why they'd send such things to me! *(tears them up)* Positively pornographic.

VICTOIRE: *(enters with card on salver)* There's a gentleman to see you both.

ANGELIQUE: A gentleman? Who?

VICTOIRE: His card!

ANGELIQUE: Ah ... Mathieu! ... Benoit! It's our friend Mathieu.

PINGLET: What? Here? From Marseilles? Send him up, Victoire.

VICTOIRE: Yes, sir.

ANGELIQUE: Clear up this mess first.

VICTOIRE: Yes, ma'am. Hotel fliers? Well, well, well.

ANGELIQUE: Off you go. Well, Mathieu!

PINGLET: Yes. It'll be nice to see him again. What a holiday. Marseilles! How kind he was to us.

ANGELIQUE: Couldn't have been more generous. Two whole weeks! And the food!

PINGLET: And he always made you feel that you were doing him the favor!

ANGELIQUE: "My home is your home." Wit, intelligence, conversation.

PINGLET: Well, he's a lawyer, my dear.

VICTOIRE: Please come in, sir.

PINGLET: Yes, come in, come in! Mathieu!

(Mathieu enters with a wet umbrella and hat. When he stutters he occasionally kicks his foot, quite violently, in order to get the word out of his mouth.)

ANGELIQUE: What a lovely surprise!

PINGLET: So nice to see you again.

ANGELIQUE: Sit. Please sit.

PINGLET: Give me your umbrella! You're soaked to the skin!

MATHIEU: My friends. I'm so ha-ha. I'm so ha-ha ...

PINGLET: What's so funny?

MATHIEU: I say ... I'm ha—happy to see you again.

ANGELIQUE: We feel the same.

MATHIEU: Do-do-do-do you remember last summer? We-we-we-we had such a good time. Shi-shi-shimmering sunsets. Pis-pis-pistachios right off the tree.

PINGLET: *(to Angelique)* What's going on?

MATHIEU: My friends, you didn't exp-exp-expect to see me?

PINGLET: Has something happened to you?

MATHIEU: Wa-waa-why d'you ask?

PINGLET: Well, I couldn't help noticing—not that it's so obvious, but you're having a little bit of difficulty ... er ... um ... er ... speaking.

ANGELIQUE: And we never, that is to say ... this, this summer we never, during the two weeks we ... er ... never ... um ... on the contrary.

MATHIEU: Ah, this summer. It was swel ... swel ... swell.

ANGELIQUE: We liked it.

MATHIEU: No—sweltering. And when it's ho-ho-ho-ho *(they laugh)* hot I can talk. But when it's raining, pi-pi-pi-pi-p ... Pinglet! When it's dam-dam-dam ...

PINGLET: Shh!

MATHIEU: *(he kicks)* Damp. I can't fu-fu-fu-function. My little we-we-we-weakness returns. I stu-stu-stutter.

ANGELIQUE AND PINGLET: Ahh ahh.

PINGLET: He's a walking barometer!

MATHIEU: Such a big pri, a big pri-predicament— for a la-la-la-lawyer.

PINGLET: How do you cope?

MATHIEU: When it rains I ask the judge if I can have a we-we-we ...

PINGLET: It helps?

MATHIEU: *(he kicks)* Week's adjournment.

ANGELIQUE: Well, dear dear Mathieu. And this year you chose to visit us!

MATHIEU: Madame, your ass ... your ass ... your assumption ...

34

PINGLET: Good!

MATHIEU: ... is correct.

MATHIEU: But your ass ... your assumptions about Marseilles were so wrong. All bull ... all bull ... all bullfighting and Boui-Boui-Bouillabaise, you said.

ANGELIQUE: I was wrong. We had a wonderful time.

MATHIEU: You sa-sa-said if ever I came to Paris I must st-st-st-stay with you.

ANGELIQUE: Of course.

PINGLET: And you must stay as long as you like— two, three days. Promise you'll stay three days.

MATHIEU: N ... n ... no.

ANGELIQUE: You must!

MATHIEU: No ... no.

PINGLET: We'll be disappointed.

MATHIEU: No ... a month.

PINGLET: That's wo ... wo ... wonderful.

ANGELIQUE: A month! We couldn't impose.

MATHIEU: I insist.

PINGLET: We're delighted.

MATHIEU: Good.

ANGELIQUE: *(aside)* A month! We only stayed two weeks.

PINGLET: There were two of us. Add it up. *(to Mathieu)* My dear Mathieu!

MATHIEU: I'm not pu-pu-pu-putting you out?

PINGLET: Not at all. We've got lots of room. And you're traveling light. You old bachelor, you.

MATHIEU: I've ... I've brought you a surprise.

PINGLET: You shouldn't have. Angelique!

ANGELIQUE: You shouldn't have! You're so, so thoughtful.

VICTOIRE: *(enters, followed by four porters, each carrying a trunk of descending size, five in all)* Madame, they're bringing in a trunk.

MATHIEU: It's mine.

PORTER: Special delivery!

MATHIEU: Oh lay ... oh lay ... oh lay ...

PORTER: Spanish is he?

PINGLET: Oh, lay it down.

MATHIEU: Thank you.

PORTER: Sir.

MATHIEU: How much?

PORTER: Forty sous.

ANGELIQUE: Dear God, what an enormous trunk.

PINGLET: Enormous.

VICTOIRE: This way! More porters, madame. More trunks!

PINGLET: More?

MATHIEU: Mine!

ANGELIQUE: Yours? One, two, three, four. What's going on?

MATHIEU: This is the little surprise.

ANGELIQUE: Surprise! You're too generous!

PINGLET: Mathieu, you shouldn't.

MATHIEU: Wh ... why?

ANGELIQUE: What can he have brought us in these? What can he have brought us?

PINGLET: Something out of this world. I mean, *five* trunks!

MATHIEU: Pi ... Pi ... Pinglet. I've got no change. Have you got a hundred sous? for this po ... po ... po ...

PINGLET: Porter?

MATHIEU: That's right.

PINGLET: Here we are! And go down to the basement and have a glass of water each.

FOUR PORTERS: Thank you, sir. *(they exit)*

PINGLET: You shouldn't have! Well, we might as well open them.

ANGELIQUE: Yes, let's open them right away.

MATHIEU: Why?

PINGLET: The surprise.

MATHIEU: No ... no ...

ANGELIQUE: He wants to keep us in suspense.

MATHIEU: You'll fu ... fu ... fu ... find out soon enough.

ANGELIQUE: The suspense is killing ... you really shouldn't have....

PINGLET: I've known a few generous men in my time, but your generosity is unpa ... unpa... unpa ... Christ! He's got me doing it. Unpa ...

MATHIEU: Unparalleled.

PINGLET AND ANGELIQUE: Well done!

MATHIEU: I never stutter for other people.

VICTOIRE: Madame, there are some young ladies here who just arrived. They are asking ...

MATHIEU: They're asking for me. Send them up.

VICTOIRE: Yes, sir.

MATHIEU: Ah ha. Surprise, surprise.

PINGLET AND ANGELIQUE: Huh?

MATHIEU: You didn't meet my daughters. Since my wife died, eight years ago, I've kept my ba-ba-ba-babies in a convent. But they had to leave. A lot of girls had mu-mu-mu ... mumps. And I took them out and said to myself, the Pi-Pi-Pinglets haven't seen my girls. So I'll give them a surprise.

PINGLET: Well.

ANGELIQUE: That's the surprise!

MATHIEU: Yes, yes, yes.

PINGLET: And the trunks?

MATHIEU: My girl's nicknacks.

ANGELIQUE AND PINGLET: Good heavens.

MATHIEU: Here they are. *(the girls enter)* Co ... co ... co ... come in.

PINGLET: Four of them.

ANGELIQUE: What a surprise! More of a shock really.

MATHIEU: Come my Pea ... pea ... pea ...

GIRLS: ... ches.

MATHIEU: Yes. How often have I spoke about the Pi ... pi ... pi ...

GIRLS: ... nglets.

MATHIEU: Yes. Well, here they are! Give them a kiss.

GIRLS: Madame Pinglet. Monsieur Pinglet.

ANGELIQUE AND PINGLET: *(resisting)* Charming, charming. But ...

ANGELIQUE: But ... it's an invasion ... an invasion.

PINGLET: Goddamn locusts.

ANGELIQUE: We didn't know you had so many daughters.

MATHIEU: *(pleased)* I was fu-fu-fu- *(he kicks, just missing Pinglet)* fertile. There they are!

PINGLET: But where will they stay?

MATHIEU: Here ... I thought.

ANGELIQUE: What?

PINGLET: Here? No, no, no. Not possible.

MATHIEU: But you told me ...

PINGLET: Yes, I told you. I told you to drop in. Not drop on! I was being ... I was being polite.

MATHIEU: Oh.

PINGLET: You took me at my word. Good! You came. Fine. But this is not a barracks.

MATHIEU: Ba-ba-ba-barracks? If it was, my daughters wouldn't be here.

PINGLET: Amazing, amazing!!! He thinks we keep a flophouse.

39

ANGELIQUE: It's your fault! "Come any time ... any time. Just drop in!"

PINGLET: My fault! It was yours. You said to me, "We've got to invite him. Two wonderful weeks!" you said. "We've got to ask him back."

ANGELIQUE: I didn't think he'd come.

PINGLET: Well, he did. He has! And it's your fault!

ANGELIQUE: Yours! If you'd just said, "Come by sometime." You know, casually. He'd never have accepted and we'd 've been off the hook. But noooo. You had to insist. Drop in.... Drop in.... Drop in. Like an inebriated parrot.... So he did. And brought the whole tribe with him.

PINGLET: Of course. My fault. *(to Mathieu)* I knew it would be my fault!

MATHIEU: Well, I understand. We have to go.

PINGLET: I'm afraid so. I have no room for all of you.

MATHIEU: Well. All right, let's go my little chika-chika-chika ...

GIRLS: ... dees.

MATHIEU: Thank the Pi-Pi-Pi-nglets for the nice welcome.

GIRLS: Thank you, monsieur. Thank you, madame.

PINGLET: Not at all. Angelique, would you see if the porters are still in the basement?—we need to get the trunks out of here.

ANGELIQUE: Right away.

MARCELLE: *(enters and bumps into the children)* What are these?

ANGELIQUE: Come in, my dear. They're on their way out.

MATHIEU: Madame!!!

PINGLET: My dear, this is Mathieu. You've heard me talk of him. Mathieu and his ... descendants. Mathieu ... Madame Paillardin! *(to her)* I've found just the place. You're still on?

MARCELLE: Yes!

PINGLET: Eight o'clock. Corner of Avenue du Bois and rue de la Pompe. Be in a carriage with the blinds down. I'll be wearing a hat and a white carnation.

MARCELLE: Why?

PINGLET: So you'll recognize me.

MARCELLE: But I know you already. *(the porters remove the trunks)*

MATHIEU: *(to Pinglet)* Pinglet, where do you think we should stay?

PINGLET: I'll be right with you.

MATHIEU: We need a hotel.

MARCELLE: Where are we going?

PINGLET: The Paradise Hotel. 220 rue de Provence.

MATHIEU: Thanks. The Paradise Hotel, 220 rue de Provence. Well, thank you. See you soon.

ANGELIQUE: Come along.

GIRLS: Bye bye, madame.

ANGELIQUE: Girls!

MARCELLE: Monsieur.

MATHIEU: Madame Paillardin, enchanted!

MARCELLE: Monsieur.

MATHIEU: Thanks. See you soon. We're off.

PINGLET: Where?

MATHIEU: To the hotel.

PINGLET: Good. Well, off you go.

ANGELIQUE: Bye bye. *(she escorts them all out)*

PINGLET: Oh, Marcelle, I'm so excited!

MARCELLE: We must be serious about this.

PINGLET: Your husband—he's gone?

MARCELLE: Yes. Hardly said goodbye. Won't know what hit him. Just wait!

PINGLET: I'm waiting!

MARCELLE: You?

PINGLET: I'm so excited. Soooo excited. My wife is going to her sister's, your husband is gone.... Let's have a little dinner together ... first. Let's go all the way!!! Dinner together ... in a restaurant!!!

MARCELLE: Yes! In a restaurant! Total revenge! I'm ready!

PINGLET: So am I. Go get ready. Half an hour. The corner of rue de la Pompe and Avenue du Bois.

MARCELLE: I'll be there.

ANGELIQUE: *(enters)* You're leaving, my dear?

MARCELLE: Yes, I have a slight headache.

ANGELIQUE: Take care of yourself. *(to Victoire)* Put it down over there, Victoire.

42

PINGLET: What's that.

ANGELIQUE: Your dinner.... Victoire has to take Maxime to the Lycee.

PINGLET: My dinner?

ANGELIQUE: Yes. That'll be all, Victoire. *(Victoire exits)*

PINGLET: Thank you, but no. On second thought, I won't dine at home tonight. You're going to your sister's. I'll be a bachelor tonight. I'll have a little meal in a restaurant.

ANGELIQUE: A restaurant?! I won't allow it! You! Have dinner in a restaurant?!

PINGLET: Why not?

ANGELIQUE: Why not? Because you're a married man. And a married man doesn't go to a restaurant without his wife.

PINGLET: I didn't know that.

ANGELIQUE: What would people think?

PINGLET: What do you think they'd think?

ANGELIQUE: The day you go to a restaurant—I'll be sitting right next to you.

PINGLET: Men will faint with envy.

ANGELIQUE: Careful, Pinglet. Tonight? Dinner. Here!

PINGLET: I've had enough. You treat me like a child. "Please, teacher, can I leave the room to go to a restaurant?"

ANGELIQUE: Stop playing the fool.

PINGLET: I've had enough, I tell you.... I'm going to a restaurant.

ANGELIQUE: No, you're not.

PINGLET: Yes, I am.

ANGELIQUE: No, you're not.

PINGLET: Yes!

ANGELIQUE: No! *(takes the door key)* And you may not leave the room.

PINGLET: You wouldn't!

ANGELIQUE: Yes, I would!

PINGLET: Give me that key. Give me that key!

ANGELIQUE: No.

PINGLET: Give it to me.

(she wallops him)

PINGLET: Yeeaw! You wouldn't ... you wouldn't. *(she leaves)*

ANGELIQUE: *(from behind door which she has bolted)* I have. Bye bye, Pinglet. See you tomorrow.

PINGLET: Locked. All locked. The old cow. But ... *(exits via the window by a rope ladder, with the cry)* into the breach!

44

ACT 2

The lobby of the Paradise Hotel. Bastien is chopping candles in half with a large cleaver.

BASTIEN: There we are. One little candle and one little candle makes four little candles. It may not seem much, but in the fifteen years I've been the manager of this hotel—and, Holy Goodness, the things I've seen, the things I've seen—in the fifteen years here in the Paradise I've made about six thousand francs by cutting candles in half. Oh, the perks. Oh, the perks. I'm not cheating them, our customers do it in the dark.

BOULOT: *(enters from upstairs)* My God, my God, my God. *My God!*

BASTIEN: Flattery will get you everywhere. Now what's the matter, Boulot? You look boolowed over. Excuse my humor....

BOULOT: If you'd seen what I've just seen.

BASTIEN: I probably have.

BOULOT: And it wasn't my fault. I did what you told me to—I knocked first....

BASTIEN: And?

BOULOT: Room 32. I knocked.

BASTIEN: And?

BOULOT: A voice said, "Come in." So I did. And there was this woman—completely naked.

45

BASTIEN: And?

BOULOT: And?! I'm telling you—a woman—completely naked. No clothes on. All her ... thingies showing.

BASTIEN: And?

BOULOT: And she said to me ... "Boy," she said, "get me a pack of cards." What would you have done if you were me?

BASTIEN: I'd have probably gotten her a pack of cards.

BOULOT: But she was all naked.

BASTIEN: And?

BOULOT: It's not natural.

BASTIEN: On the contrary. Naked as a jaywalker is how we came into the world. A naked woman is very natural in the hotel business.

BOULOT: Life in the suburbs is very different from Paris.

BASTIEN: Boulot, we're going to have to desuburbanize you. In two weeks, you'll see a naked pair of ... and you won't bat a hair or turn an eye. Take life with a lump of salt like me. Do me a favor. Go and knock on number 9.

BOULOT: Number 9? What do you think she'll be wearing?

BASTIEN: There's no woman in number 9. It's that pinhead Chervet. That pinhead schoolmaster. The boss says he hasn't paid a bill in weeks. So out he goes and ... we keep his trunk, just to be sure. Go and tell him he's out of here.

BOULOT: Me?

BASTIEN: Yes, you.

BOULOT: Monsieur Chervet? The loony with the terrible temper! Always shouting, "I'll blow your brains out. I'll blow your brains out!"

BASTIEN: It's just a turn of the phrase.

BOULOT: But what if he blows my brains out?

BASTIEN: File a report and I'll take care of it. Off you go.

BOULOT: Yes, Monsieur Bastien. I get the worst jobs.

(knocks)

CHERVET: Come in, you son of a bitch.

BOULOT: I prefer number 32, and the nice lady with ... *(goes in)* and no clothes on....

BASTIEN: Poor kid. He'll toughen up in fifteen years.... *(a bell)* I love that sound.

(Antoinette and Ernest, who is very drunk, enter)

ANTOINETTE: Bellboy?

BASTIEN: Yes, madame? What would the lady and gentleman desire this evening?

ANTOINETTE: Do you have a ...

BASTIEN: Room available? Yes, madame, there is. A little love nest away from home, where love can blossom and no questions asked. He's a lucky man and a handsome man, and madame is beautiful. Very good taste.

ANTOINETTE: Keep your eyes on the books, buddy.

BASTIEN: Madame has a wonderful sense of humor!

ANTOINETTE: Shut it.

47

BASTIEN: Don't I recognize you, madame? Antoinette from the Theatre de la Chanson? Well known for your rotating repertory....

ANTOINETTE: Keep it down! He's a Duke.

BASTIEN: Understood, madame. We are the soul of discretion. Oh, you're in luck tonight. Room 22 is available. The Barrault twins usually operate out of there.

ANTOINETTE: Oh.

BASTIEN: But I'm sure that one madame in the hand is worth two of them in the bushes.

ANTOINETTE: Whatever that means....

ERNEST: Is there any difficulty?

ANTOINETTE: No, no, my darling....

BASTIEN: I hope you like the room, madame. Implements are extra.

ANTOINETTE: So you recognized me!

BASTIEN: Everybody knows of you. What comes around goes around.

ANTOINETTE: No, he's a Duke.

BASTIEN: Congratulations! So you really should take Room 22. When his Royal Highness the Grand Prince of Poland came here for his honeymoon night, that's where he slept. With his chambermaid. Your Duke will feel right at home, like a duck in the water.

ANTOINETTE: We've got a royal suite.... *(yells and screams from upstairs)* What's that noise?

BASTIEN: Nothing. It's just a customer we have to be disposing of.... *(gunshot)*

BOULOT: *(enters)* Ay ay ayyyy. I told you.... I told you he'd blow my brains out. He won't go until you give him back his trunk.

BASTIEN: Won't go? We'll see about that. Chervet! Chervet! Come here a minute.

CHERVET: *(enters)* What do you want.

BASTIEN: You see those stairs, sir? Do me a favor. Take a nice walk down those stairs and get the hell out of the front door.

CHERVET: I won't go till I get my trunk.

BASTIEN: You won't get your trunk till I get paid.

CHERVET: Oh yeah? Well I have influence in the Police Department—Morals Division. Perhaps you'll change your tune when the police arrive.

ERNEST: Police?!

ANTOINETTE: Here?!

CHERVET: Yeah, police. I would tell them a thing or two about this place. The way it's run, madame— it's a scandal.

ANTOINETTE: What do you mean?

BASTIEN: When you've quite finished, Chervet!

CHERVET: I'm not talking to you.... I'm talking to the lady. I mean ... this isn't a hotel, it's a flea-pit!

BASTIEN: That is not a true fact.... We spray ... on a daily basis.... Top-grade powder.

CHERVET: It chokes the guests, and it's very popular with the fleas. Furthermore, madame—the place is haunted.

ERNEST: Haunted?

BASTIEN: Will you please put a cork up it, Monsieur Chervet?

CHERVET: And that room's the worst.... *(pointing to room 22)* Ghosts in there every night. Wham ... bang ... thump ... thump ... thump....

ERNEST: How dreadful!

BASTIEN: It's not a true fact, I tell you!

CHERVET: Not a true fact? Can you deny that there's an expert coming here tonight ... an expert from the Sanitation Department?

ERNEST: An expert? *(overlapping)*

ANTOINETTE: This is no place for us—give number 22 back to the twins!

BASTIEN: Madame is leaving?

ANTOINETTE: Madame is leaving like a rocket.... Wait, your highness.... *(they exit)*

BASTIEN: But madame ... *(to Chervet)* This is your fault!

CHERVET: Yes ... they've gone, and I'm going too. ...Buuuuut ... you will be hearing from me. ...*(cocking his finger like a gun at Boulot)* And you'll be hearing from me, too. *(exits)*

BASTIEN: Good riddance.... You'll be kicked out of worse places than this!

BOULOT: We lost two clients because of him.

BASTIEN: Clients! Don't talk to me about clients! ... I'm sick of them.... All the same, I would like to have watched that Antoinette "de la Chanson" rotating her repertory with a live Duke.

BOULOT: Watched? How? Perhaps they wouldn't have asked you in.

BASTIEN: Asked me in! Oh, the boy has the brain of a chick-pea! I'd have watched them ... I'd have watched them!

BOULOT: How?

BASTIEN: The boy's a mango.... *(takes drill from under desk)* You know what this is?

BOULOT: A drill ... for making holes.

BASTIEN: What a brain ... yes ... when a client is tickling my fancy ... I am making the hole ... and I am getting an eyeful....

BOULOT: No?

BASTIEN: Yes.... I've seen some of the most beautiful women in Paris ... through the holes.... *(bell rings)*

PAILLARDIN: Manager ... manager, please!

BASTIEN: Here we are, sir.... You are expecting someone? I know just what the gentleman needs—a little love nest away from home, where love can blossom and no questions asked....

PAILLARDIN: No, thank you ... I'm not expecting anyone ... you are expecting me! I am Monsieur Paillardin—the learned architectural expert assigned by the Board of Sanitation.

BASTIEN: Ah, yes, the expert.... You've come about the haunted room. Sir! A veritable witches' brewery! *(a bell)* Boulot! Move! A customer is ringing upstairs.... Every night, sir, pandemonium! The walls crack! Chairs jump up in the air!

PAILLARDIN: Yes ... yes ... I'm sure they do. Good.

Well, since I'm here as an expert investigator, I won't be needing your superstitious explanations, thank you. Where's the room?

BASTIEN: This one here, sir. A candle for you, sir? *(Bastien lights a candle, then they enter room 22)*

PAILLARDIN: Well, let's take a look at the haunted chamber!

BASTIEN: This is it, sir. And rather you than me to be staying here tonight.

PAILLARDIN: *(laughing)* This is it? Strangely quiet for a witches' brewery! *(laughs)*

BASTIEN: Quiet at this time, sir.

PAILLARDIN: Ghosts gone out to dinner, have they? *(laughs)*

BASTIEN: *(faint chuckle)* But when the hour comes, then, sir, in the darkness, the terror begins. It's like a drunken brawl.

PAILLARDIN: High spirits, eh?

BASTIEN: Sir will have his little joke. But Monsieur The Expert will be laughing on the other side of his face.

(someone is singing upstairs)

PAILLARDIN: Warming up, are they? Singing spirituals? *(laughs)*

BASTIEN: It's some stock boys from the department store. Every weekend here with the sales girls. We can't always control them, sir. But they're young. I'll get them to keep quiet.

PAILLARDIN: All right, all right. Now ... my cigars, hair brushes. *(he unpacks his combs and brushes)*

BASTIEN: Hey, you up there! Cut it out!

VOICE: *(raspberry)*

BASTIEN: I'll give you *(raspberry)*. I'm coming up.

(Pinglet and Marcelle enter the lobby. Bastien rushes past them.)

PINGLET: Excuse me ...

BASTIEN: In a minute, sir. With you in a minute.

PINGLET: In a minute—he'll be with us in a minute. Looks like a nice respectable hotel. We're lucky, I think.

MARCELLE: It's a ... it's horrible, your hotel! Where did you find a place like this?

PINGLET: Perhaps there's a certain lack of elegance. But it's just what we wanted. I mean, in a first-class establishment we might be recognized. But here! Not a chance of meeting anyone we know.

MARCELLE: That's true.

PAILLARDIN: *(in room 22)* Aaaaaacchhoooo!

PINGLET: Bless you.

PAILLARDIN: Thank you. *(he goes into his bathroom with his candle, and room 22 goes dark)*

PINGLET: You're welcome. Anyway, who cares about the hotel? It looks beautiful to me, as long as I'm with you. Geez. Can you smell that? It's like drains or something. Ah. Here's the manager.

BASTIEN: Here we are, sir, at your service. I know what the gentleman needs. A little love nest away from home, where love can blossom and

53

no questions asked. And your madame is very beautiful too, sir. Very beautiful!

PINGLET: Not so familiar, please. In any case, madame is my wife.

BASTIEN: No!

PINGLET: Yes, she is!

BASTIEN: No, she's not!

PINGLET: How can you tell?

BASTIEN: Monsieur is carrying the bag. *(Pinglet gives Marcelle her bag)*

PINGLET: The man's a mystic. Do you have anything to offer on this floor?

BASTIEN: Yes, sir. Oh, you are in luck tonight. Number 10 is available. This was the room in which His Royal Highness the Grand Prince of Poland spent his honeymoon night ... with his chambermaid.

PINGLET: Perfect. Perfect. *(to Marcelle)* We're getting the room where the Prince of Poland spent his honeymoon with ... you'll love it. I told you it was respectable.

(They enter room 10. Bastien carries their candle and puts it on a table.)

BASTIEN: Here we are, sir. A night in Paradise. Your very own fireplace. All modern conveniences, including a bathroom for your every need. You'll be as snug as a bug in a rug.

PINGLET: Unfortunate turn of phrase. I'll take it. *(to Marcelle)* Oh ... Marcelle....

MARCELLE: Shhh. He's still here.

PINGLET: That's fine. I told you I'd take the room.

BASTIEN: Good night, madame. Good night, sir.
(he exits)

PINGLET: Good night. *(to Marcelle)* Marcelle!

(Bastien returns)

BASTIEN: The key, sir. And all my good wishes.
(exits to lobby)

(Paillardin is on his way out)

BASTIEN: Going out, sir?

PAILLARDIN: Yes, it's too early really to go to bed. I'll
have a beer in the cafe next door. Be back in
half an hour.

BASTIEN: Very good, sir. Your candle will be waiting.
(he exits from lobby)

(in their room ...)

PINGLET: *(with cigar in his mouth)* Marcelle.

MARCELLE: Pinglet.

PINGLET: Not Pinglet, don't call me Pinglet any
more. Call me ... Benoit.

MARCELLE: All right. Benoit.

PINGLET: Yes, Benoit. Oh, Marcelle. The hour of
vengeance is upon us, Marcelle ... in my arms.
(tries to grab her)

MARCELLE: Careful. You'll burn me with that cigar.

PINGLET: Wait. Marcelle, I love you.

MARCELLE: You'll set me on fire.

PINGLET: I hope so, I hope so.... Oh, I'm sorry!

MARCELLE: Could you put it out please?

PINGLET: It cost forty sous. I'd like to finish it.

MARCELLE: Go ahead then.

PINGLET: Damn the expense. *(puts the cigar out)* When one's in love, money is nothing. You are so beautiful.

MARCELLE: Do you like my dress?

PINGLET: You'd look beautiful in anything. Or in nothing at all.

MARCELLE: Pinglet. Pinglet. It only came this evening. You're the first one to see it on me.

PINGLET: But let's not talk about the dress. It's just the wrapper, and you're my chocolate truffle. You could do without it, my little Godiva. I want you. I want you. I want to gobble you up. *(he grabs her in his arms, they fall, she retreats)*

MARCELLE: Good heavens!! What's the matter with you. Get a hold of yourself, Benoit.

PINGLET: I want you, I tell you, I want you!!

MARCELLE: What's the matter? I've never seen you like this, Pinglet. Stop it. Monsieur Benoit, the champagne has gone to your head.

PINGLET: It's not the champagne. It's you. You've gone to my head. It's the dinner, the wine, the liqueurs, the cigar. My wife doesn't let me smoke and she doesn't let me drink. Says they'll make me ill. Never felt better in my life. I want you, I want you.

(Takes her in his arms. Sits on a chair which collapses.)

PINGLET: Ooh la la ... Stupid. Stupid. Stupid chair.

MARCELLE: You look so funny like that.

PINGLET: *(aside)* Go ahead. Laugh at me.

MARCELLE: You're not hurt, are you?

PINGLET: No, not at all. I'm fine, fine. Goddamn chair. And there's only one. They could have left a sturdier one.

(throws the chair out into the lobby)

PINGLET: Now. Where were we? Oh yes.... Ah, Marcelle.

MARCELLE: If you could have seen yourself ...

PINGLET: Please, Marcelle, stop laughing.

MARCELLE: You looked so cute!

PINGLET: There was nothing funny about it.

MARCELLE: *(handkerchief in mouth)* No, you're right. Nothing, nothing.

BOULOT: *(enters into lobby)* That's the chair from number 10.

PINGLET: Marcelle, my darling.

BOULOT: What's it doing here? *(goes in)* Oh!

PINGLET AND MARCELLE: Oh!

BOULOT: Oh, excuse me, sir! I didn't know this room was occupied. I was just returning this chair.

PINGLET: No. No. I don't want to see that chair again. I don't want to see you again. Take it out! Take it out!

BOULOT: But sir, it belongs in this room.

PINGLET: Out! Out! Out!

BOULOT: She's delicious, that little lady. I wonder. ...Well, why not! I'll get the drill.

57

BASTIEN: *(upstairs)* Boulot! Boulot!

BOULOT: Coming. Coming. *(he exits with chair)*

PINGLET *(worried):* Oh, my God! Ooh, I feel ... I feel strange.

MARCELLE: What's the matter?

PINGLET: Not sure. Like a cold sweat. It's gone to my head. Feel dizzy. I must be overly excited ... it's nothing. *(takes her in his arms)* Ah, Marcelle! Here we are ... alone at last ... in each other's arms. I wish you could see what's going on deep inside me. I feel my heart ... my heart ... oh, my God! Phwo ... my heart is ... beating ... hard.

MARCELLE: You've gone all white, Pinglet. Benoit! Benoit! You poor thing, are you all right?

PINGLET: Whwoo, I feel sick ... it's throbbing.... I feel quite sick.

MARCELLE: Sit down. There we go. Sit down.

PINGLET: Where, there's no chair.

MARCELLE: Well, sit on the table.

PINGLET: Oh, Marcelle ... forgive me, I'm so sorry about all this. The most wonderful moment of my life and ... but it will go away. It'll go. Ooh la la. Oh oh oh.

MARCELLE: Hold on! I'll get you some water.

PINGLET: It was the cigar. I told you it was the cigar. But it will go away. And the champagne.... I only drink water. Normally. Yes, the cigar and the champagne. Ooh la la. Oh oh oh. *(getting up)*

MARCELLE: You poor thing!

PINGLET: Oh, my God! I wish my wife were here!

MARCELLE: Now don't get up. Sit. Sit.

PINGLET: I can't. No. I've got to walk around. I've got to get out of here.

MARCELLE: I'll come with you.

PINGLET: No. No. By myself. I think I'd better go by myself. I need some air. Suffocating.

MARCELLE: Take off your jacket.

PINGLET: Yes. Good idea. Yes. Ohh la la.

MARCELLE: Come on now. Steady. Sit down.

(Pinglet sits on the table with his back to the wall)

PINGLET: Oh, Marcelle, something tells me that ... I think I'm going to die.

MARCELLE: No no.

PINGLET: Right here.

MARCELLE: Don't say things like that. *(she wipes his forehead with a kerchief)* Not right here.

BOULOT: *(outside, with drill)* I mean, why not. Bastien does it all the time. *(testing wall)*

PINGLET: Thank you.

BOULOT: Where would be the best place? That part seems soft enough.

PINGLET: Thank you.

BOULOT: This seems good.

PINGLET: *(leaning)* You're so good to me.

BOULOT: Just a little hole. Teeny weeny one. Right there. They won't suspect a thing.

MARCELLE: Is that better?

PINGLET: Not much. Mmmm ... mmmmm ... *(he's enjoying the tickling sensation)* mmmm....

BOULOT: There we go. Like a knife through butter.

PINGLET: Yeeaaw. My God, what was that!

MARCELLE: What's the matter?

PINGLET: I don't know. A stabbing pain. Right at the base of my spine.

MARCELLE: That's a good sign. Your circulation's working again.

PINGLET: *(the drill pierces a second time)* Yeeaaw.

MARCELLE: What is it?

PINGLET: *(leaping from wall)* Wha. Ooh la la.

BOULOT: That's got it.

PINGLET: Wha. Ooh la la.

MARCELLE: What's the matter with you?

PINGLET: I don't know. It was like a sharp stabbing pain.... Like someone was poking holes in me.

MARCELLE: Where?

PINGLET: *(pointing to his rump)* Down there.

MARCELLE: Oh, my God, perhaps it's a cerebral hemorrhage. I think we'd better get a doctor.

PINGLET: No no, I just want some air. *(he fans himself with her hat)* And maybe some camomile tea.

BOULOT: Let's have a look-see.

PINGLET: *(opening door)* Boy!

BOULOT: Oh, my God.

PINGLET: What are you doing down there?

BOULOT: I thought I heard you call, sir, so I was just listening.

PINGLET: *(tiny voice)* Boy ... I need a balcony. I must have some air.

BOULOT: One flight up, sir. Turn at the end of the corridor.

PINGLET: Thank you.

MARCELLE: *(in doorway)* Go get a hot water bottle for the gentleman.

PINGLET: Yes, get me a hot water bottle. You'll wait for me, won't you?

MARCELLE: Yes.

PINGLET: Oh, God, I feel sick. I feel sick. *(exits upstairs)*

MARCELLE: Poor thing. Quick, get some camomile tea, any sort of tea, so long as it's camomile.

BOULOT: The kitchen is closed, madame—at this time of night. Wait a minute. *(he goes to Chervet's room)* The fellow upstairs used to make his own tea every night. He should have all that equipment in here.

MARCELLE: Oh, my God, what a night.

BOULOT: *(returning)* Here we are, madame, I knew I'd find all you needed.

MARCELLE: Good. Put it down.

BOULOT: Yes, madame.

MARCELLE: Is he all right, do you think? Won't he catch cold out there on the balcony?

BOULOT: *(lighting the spirit lamp under the kettle)* No, madame, I'm sure he'll be fine. It's nice out. Not like this morning. Never seen such rain. It's a beautiful night out there ... a full moon, not a cloud in the sky.

MATHIEU: *(entering the lobby)* Come along, children, come along.

GIRLS: Yes, papa. Here we are.

MATHIEU: Well, where's the porter? I don't see a porter. I've never seen a hotel like this. It's open house down there. Anyone can walk in. No doorman. We could have been burglars. No one would care. We could have been housebreakers or bandits or assassins or cutthroats. We could be tearing the place apart, pillaging, robbing, plundering, sacking the very foundations. I mean, what's the desk bell for?

PAQUERETTE: It's stopped raining.

MATHIEU: I don't know why Pinglet recommended this place. It's a seedy, smelly old dump.

PERVENCHE: It's icky.

GIRLS: Oooo....

MATHIEU: But it's late. We'll have to spend the night here. We'll leave our luggage downstairs and find somewhere really nice tomorrow.

MARGARITE: I just love a good hotel ... silk sheets ...cute bellboys.

GIRLS: Me too, me too, me too.

MARCELLE: *(to Boulot)* The kettle has boiled. There we are. You can go now. Don't forget the hot water bottle. *(she goes into her bathroom, taking her candle with her, and the room darkens)*

BOULOT: Yes, madame. Gorgeous! ... and stuck with an invalid like that. Ooh la. *(exits to lobby)*

MATHIEU: Aah! The porter!

BOULOT: What do you think this is? A girls camp?

MATHIEU: Now look here, boy, we came here on the personal recommendation of Monsieur Pinglet.

BOULOT: Oh, Monsieur Pinglet? Of course ... *(aside)* never heard of him.

MATHIEU: Well, my boy, I need rooms for my daughters and myself.

BOULOT: His daughters! Are these your daughters? ... *(aside)* breeds like a rabbit.

MATHIEU: Now what can you give us?

BOULOT: *(looking at the keys)* Let's see ... well, I don't have enough room for all of ... *(aside)* of course, the haunted room. It's empty! Always. Well, sir, if you're not too picky, I think I might have something available.

MATHIEU: We'll take a look.

BOULOT: *(with candle)* Here we are, sir, the presidential suite. *(they enter room 22)*

MATHIEU: It's a dormitory.

BOULOT: It's all we've got, sir, just at the moment. Four girls. You. Five beds.

MATHIEU: I can't sleep in the same room as my daughters.

BOULOT: Jump into bed first and close the curtains when they're undressing. And I can offer separate toilet facilities. At no extra charge.

GIRLS: Oooooo....

63

MATHIEU: We've got no choice, I guess. How much do you charge for this ... presidential suite?

BOULOT: Well, sir, under the circumstances, seeing you were sent by Monsieur ... uh Monsieur ... Thinglet ... personally ... how about seven francs. No extras.

MATHIEU: Well, that's pretty reasonable.

MARCELLE: *(coming out of her bathroom)* I wonder how Pinglet is doing. Where *is* he?

MATHIEU: We'll take the room. *(he puts his candle on Paillardin's cigar box)*

BOULOT: Very good, sir. Good night, sir. Good night, young ladies.

MARGARITE: Good night, Monsieur Porter.

MARCELLE: Perhaps he's really ill. Oh, my God, I'm getting worried.

MATHIEU: I need a candle for my girls.

(both Marcelle and Mathieu go to the landing and say together ...)

MARCELLE AND MATHIEU: Porter! Before you go!

MARCELLE: Monsieur Mathieu!

MATHIEU: If I'm not mistaken it's ... why ... Madame Paillardin!?

MARCELLE: *(turning away)* No, I'm not. No. Well, yes ... as a matter of fact.

MATHIEU: I had the distinct pleasure of meeting you this morning at the house of our mutual friend, Monsieur Pinglet.

MARCELLE: The pleasure was mine. Really.

64

BOULOT: They know each other.

MATHIEU: What a wonderful surprise. *(shouts)* Girls!

MARCELLE: Please, not now.

MATHIEU: They'd love to see you. Girls, look who's here. Madame Paillardin.

MARCELLE: Oh, my God, he's shouting my name out.

MATHIEU: Remember this morning? Madame Paillardin!

MARCELLE: All over the place.

BOULOT: Aah ... Madame Paillardin.

GIRLS: Madame Paillardin. Madame Paillardin. What a surprise, it's Madame Paillardin. *(they surround her, jumping up and down with excitement)*

MARCELLE: Please God! This is all I need.

BOULOT: *(shouts from her room)* Madame Paillardin. Tea's ready.

MARCELLE: Wonderful! He knows my name. Great. My tea, thank you.

MATHIEU: Your tea? I don't ... do you live here?

MARCELLE: Me? Er, no. That is to say, yes. My husband's idea. We're buying a bigger house and, you know, the movers.... So for the time being ... er ... yes.

VIOLET: We're right next door to you.

GIRLS: We're so happy.

BOULOT: Madame Paillardin. Tea's ready.

MARCELLE: I'll kill him. I'll kill him.

BOULOT: Madame Paillardin, tea's ready.

MARCELLE: Thank you. *(to Mathieu)* I'm so sorry ... but you understand ... my tea. Love to have had you join me ... another time perhaps?

MATHIEU: *(overlapping her last line)* We'd love to.

GIRLS: Oh yes.

MATHIEU: It'd be a pleasure.

GIRLS: ... Tea tea tea tea.

MARCELLE: Aaagh.

MATHIEU: Porter, cups!

BOULOT: Yes, sir.

MATHIEU: Come along, girls, we're going to pay a visit to Madame Paillardin.

MARCELLE: His jacket! *(hides it behind her)*

MATHIEU: *(looking around)* Very nice. Very nice indeed.

MARCELLE: *(in bathroom)* Yes. Isn't it.

MATHIEU: Come on, girls.

MARCELLE: *(re-entering)* Won't you sit down?

MATHIEU: How kind. But I perceive there is a slight paucity of seating apparatus.

MARCELLE: *(forced laugh)* How very true ... he does have a way with words.

BOULOT: *(returning with tray)* Cups.

GIRLS: Tea tea tea tea.

PAQUERETTE: Finally.

MATHIEU: Now, chairs! Porter, chairs!

BOULOT: *(going to Chervet's room)* Yes, sir.

66

MATHIEU: Give him a hand, girls. Off you go. *(they follow and return with chairs)*

MARCELLE: Oh, my God, how can I get rid of them? And Pinglet will be down any minute. I know it, I know it.

MATHIEU: Now, madame, if I may, a little hot water in the pot.

MARCELLE: Now he's cooking. Please!

MATHIEU: How do you like your tea, madame?

MARCELLE: Hot.

BOULOT: Chairs.

MARCELLE: It's Pinglet's fault. It's Pinglet's fault. Pinglet. Pinglet. What a stupid name.

BOULOT: I'll get the hot water bottle now.

MARCELLE: What water bottle?

BOULOT: For the invalid upstairs.

MARCELLE: Ah yes, yes. Go. Now. *(aside)* Maybe suicide?... Please, sit down. Please, sit down. *(they're already seated)*

MATHIEU: We have. Is anything the matter, Madame Paillardin?

MARCELLE: Oh no. Nothing, nothing.

MATHIEU: Come on, girls! Manners, manners. Serve the tea. And our old friend Pinglet, do you see him often? *(the girls serve the tea)*

MARCELLE: Oh, not very often. You know how Paris is. You never see your neighbors. Of course, Madame Pinglet and I are very close. We're like this. That's why I was there this morning.

PINGLET: *(on the landing)* I feel better. I feel better. The fresh air was wonderful and I said goodbye to my dinner. Over the balcony. I'm ready for action ... for romance.
In your arms
My cheek next to yours
In your arms
As we dance.

MATHIEU: So, not very often.

MARCELLE: No, not very often.

(Pinglet waltzes into the room)

GIRLS: *(shout)* Monsieur Pinglet.

PINGLET: The Mathieus.

MARCELLE: Suicide.

PINGLET: What are they doing here?

MATHIEU: Pinglet Pinglet. We were just talking about you.

ALL: Yes, yes, we were.

PINGLET: How nice of you. Oh ... Madame Paillardin! Good evening. How are you? I ... er ... had some business to attend to in this part of town. And I thought I'd just pop in to say hello to Madame Paillardin.

MARCELLE: How kind of you. What a surprise.

GIRLS: Yes, yes.

MATHIEU: But do you always go out in your shirt sleeves?

PINGLET: Yes ... er ... I mean no. I mean my ... er ... jacket was torn so I took it to a tailor ... er ... down the street and ... while he was fixing it I thought I'd just pop in to say hello to Madame Paillardin.

MARCELLE: How kind of you. What a surprise.

GIRLS: Yes, yes.

PINGLET: *(to Marcelle)* So ... hello.

MARCELLE: *(to Pinglet)* Hello.

VIOLET: A cup of tea, Monsieur Pinglet?

PINGLET: Tea? Oh, yes, thank you so much.

MARGARITE: Sugar, Monsieur Pinglet?

PINGLET: Oh, yes, thank you so much. *(keeps putting lumps in his tea)* Well, well, well. I'm having tea, here, with the Mathieus.

MARGARITE: You like your tea very sweet, Monsieur Pinglet.

PINGLET: No, not too much sugar, thank you.

MARGARITE: *(giggles)*

MATHIEU: Well ... what's the news in Paris.

PINGLET: *(drinking tea)* Yeack ... *(spits it out)* news? Well, we've had a revolution ... some time ago, actually.

MATHIEU: And your wife? She's doing well? Since this morning?

PINGLET: Very well. Yes. And yours?

MATHIEU: I told you she's been dead for eight years.

PINGLET: You did. Yes. So there's not much point in asking, really. Yes. *(aside)* Why don't they just go!

MARCELLE: *(aside)* Why don't they just go!

69

BOULOT: *(enters)* Your hot water bottle, sir.

MARCELLE: That's all we need.

PINGLET: Perfect timing. *(the bottle is hot)* Yeeow.

MATHIEU: *Your* hot water bottle?

PINGLET: Not mine, no. That is to say ... yes. I mean ... every time I come here, to this hotel, I always put in an order for ... a hot water bottle.

MATHIEU: Ah.

PINGLET: Oh, yes, they're famous for their ... er ... hot water bottles. Famous. You didn't know that? Oh, yes. My wife always says to me, "If ever you're near the Paradise Hotel, pop in and get me a hot water bottle." Doesn't she say that always, Madame Paillardin?

MARCELLE: Oh, yes. Yes. Always.

BOULOT: But monsieur ...

PINGLET: That's enough. We don't need you anymore. Out. Out.

BOULOT: What? Very well, monsieur.

PINGLET: Madame Paillardin, I see that you are very tired— *(shouts)* she's tired. And I will not take up another moment of your precious time. So if you will excuse me ...

MARCELLE: *(yawning)* Well, to be quite honest ...

MATHIEU: You're tired? You should have told us. Girls! Back to our room. Manners! Manners! *(takes chair)* You should have told us.

PINGLET: *(to Marcelle)* I knew that would get to him.

MATHIEU: Good night, madame. Sleep well.

PINGLET: She will.

GIRLS: Night. *(they each take a chair)*

PINGLET: *(pushing them out)* Yes, night! Out we go! *(chairs get entangled)* Watch what you're doing! *(to Marcelle)* I'll go down to the lobby. That will put him off. I'll be right back.

MARCELLE: I don't believe this. I just don't believe this.

MATHIEU: Good night, Pinglet. Give my best to Madame Pinglet.

PINGLET: *(giving him the chair)* Oh, I will. Yes, I will. Oh, my God!

MATHIEU: *(into room)* Well now.

MARCELLE: *(in her room)* I've had enough. Eee—nough. Never again. Never again.

GIRLS: Good night, papa.

VIOLET: We're going to get undressed now.

MATHIEU: Oh, very well. There is the ... er ... um ...toilet. But don't make a noise. People are trying to sleep.

MARCELLE: I'm not going to spend a minute longer in this damned hotel. When Pinglet comes back ... *(puts on coat)*

MATHIEU: It'll be nice to get into bed ...

MARCELLE: My hat! Where's my hat?

MATHIEU: ... after such a long day.

MARCELLE: *(takes candle with her to the bathroom)* Perhaps I put it in here with Pinglet's jacket. *(darkness)*

MATHIEU: I think we're going to be just fine in

here. This room has a comfortable feel to it. I like it. Holy ... ! Look at this. First-class service, tortoise-shell combs, ebony brushes. H.P. H.P.? P.H.? Oh. Paradise Hotel. Of course. *(brushes hair)* Why not? They certainly think of everything. Hotels in Paris are miles better than in Marseilles. Now for a little cigar before bed. *(takes out a small one)* Small but tasty. *(sees cigar box)* What's this? A box of cigars? Incredible. Regalias! ... Eighty centimes apiece. *(puts his cigar away)* What a hotel! Seven francs a day and a full box of cigars! *(takes a few)* Fantastic place! No wonder Pinglet recommended it.

MARCELLE: It's gone. Amazing. I can't find my hat.

MATHIEU: Wonderful cigar! I don't see how they break even.

MARCELLE: Pinglet, where are you?! What's he doing?!

MATHIEU: *And* a nightshirt. *And* slippers. They think of everything. Fantastic.

(Pinglet returns with hot water bottle)

MARCELLE: That must be him. Let's have a look.

PINGLET: *(whispering at door)* I'm back.

MATHIEU: I want one of those hot water bottles.... *(opens his door)*

MARCELLE: Quick. Hurry up. *(Marcelle shuts door in Pinglet's face when she sees Mathieu)*

PINGLET: Mathieu!

MATHIEU: You're back!

PINGLET: Yes. I'm back. I came back ... to see you. I wanted to ask you ... er ...

MATHIEU: What?

PINGLET: Well ... um ... since I was in the neighbor-
hood I thought ...

MATHIEU: Of course.

PINGLET: Well, I was in the ... ah ... lobby and I
heard some people talking and ... uh ... they were
saying that it got pretty damn hot in the house
of representatives this afternoon.

MATHIEU: *(bored)* Oh, really?

PINGLET: Oh, yes. There were questions raised ...
about the budget. They said that the govern-
ment was just about out.

MATHIEU: Really.

PINGLET: What are things coming to? My God!
What are things coming to? So I said to myself
... got to ask Mathieu about this. He'll know
what to do.

MATHIEU: Me? What am I supposed to do about it?

PINGLET: Well, if you don't know what to do ... I
might as well go. Right now. Good night.

MATHIEU: Thanks for thinking of me. Good night!

PINGLET: Not at all! Any time! You can go back in
now ... back in!

MATHIEU: I'm waiting for the porter. I want a hot
water bottle. The hotel is famous for them.

PINGLET: Take mine. Take mine. *(gives him the hot
water bottle)*

MATHIEU: Oh, I couldn't. I wouldn't dream of
taking ...

PINGLET: I don't want it anymore. I'll pop in another time and get one.

MATHIEU: You're too kind.

PINGLET: It's nothing. You can go back in now.

MATHIEU: Yes. Good night. *(he stays)*

PINGLET: Good night. Good night.

MATHIEU: *(waving goodbye)* Good night.

PINGLET: Good night now. You can go back in now. *(aside)* Pain in the ass. *(smiles)* Good night. *(he leaves)*

MATHIEU: I like Pinglet. *(leaves)* Oh, my candle. *(face to face)* Back again!

PINGLET: I forgot to shake your hand.

MATHIEU: *(in room)* Time to get undressed. *(He goes into his bathroom. The girls are in theirs.)*

PINGLET: Ooooh. *(he goes into room 10)*

MARCELLE: Finally! I though you'd never get here.

PINGLET: My love, I had to get rid of Mathieu. It wasn't easy.

MARCELLE: Yes, this is a perfect time to talk about Mathieu.

PINGLET: I'm sorry. There must be hundreds of hotels in Paris and they pick this one. Why me?

MARCELLE: Why not. We're wasting time. Get your jacket and let's get out of here.

PINGLET: Where is it?

MARCELLE: In there.

PINGLET: Yes.

MARCELLE: Oh, and my hat. What did you do with it?

PINGLET: What do you mean, your hat? It should be here.

MARCELLE: Where where where?

PINGLET: Where where where? I don't know. You put it on the bed—no I think I took it upstairs. I must have left it on the balcony. *(he giggles)*

MARCELLE: It's not funny. What did you do that for? I mean, why take a woman's hat? Oooh la. Go get it. Birdbrain! I'll wait here.

PINGLET: Yes, wait for me.

MARCELLE: Then go, hurry up.

PINGLET: *(bumps into Bastien)* Oh.

BASTIEN: Oh, where are you going, sir?

PINGLET: I know where. I know where.

BASTIEN: I'm glad to hear it.

MARCELLE: I've had enough, more than enough.

BASTIEN: *(bell rings)* Good, good. More customers. *(Paillardin enters)* Aah, it's Monsieur The Learned Expert.

PAILLARDIN: In person.

BASTIEN: Monsieur The Learned Expert is going to bed?

PAILLARDIN: Unless that's inconvenient for you? My candle, please.

BASTIEN: Here it is, Monsieur The Learned Expert.

PAILLARDIN: And has Monsieur The Learned Bogey-Man shown up yet?

BASTIEN: Not so far as I know, Monsieur The Learned Expert.

PAILLARDIN: What a pity! Maybe he was caught in traffic.

BASTIEN: You will be laughing on the other side of your mouth pretty soon.

PAILLARDIN: Well, here we are. *(they enter room 22)* The haunted room! Bogey-bogey-bogey. Seems quite ordinary to me. Well, I hope your ghosts are quiet and well behaved. I need to get some sleep.

BASTIEN: They probably heard you say that, Monsieur The Expert.

PAILLARDIN: Hey! My cigars!

BASTIEN: Monsieur The Expert?

PAILLARDIN: My cigars! The box was full when I went out. Half of them are gone. Where are they?

BASTIEN: I have no idea.

PAILLARDIN: Of course not. Well, they didn't walk out of here.

BASTIEN: I know what it is. It's the ghosts.

PAILLARDIN: Ghosts! Don't make me laugh. Ghosts don't smoke.

BASTIEN: I don't see why not. You smoke.

PAILLARDIN: Look at this—my comb, my brushes . . . all messed up.

BASTIEN: Very observant, sir . . . eyes like a goose.

PAILLARDIN: I'm beginning to realize what kind of ghosts you have here. Some two-bit thief who passes himself off as a bogey-man. There are no ghosts.

BASTIEN: Don't count your chickens with a hatchet.

PAILLARDIN: Fine. Good. You can go. I'll have a word with your superior in the morning.

BASTIEN: Very good, sir, Good night, sir. *(exits)*

PAILLARDIN: Good night.

BASTIEN: I hope one of his bogey-men gives Monsieur a learned boink on his expert coink.

PAILLARDIN: There's a thief. It's obvious, there's a thief and he left his dirty hair on my brush.

PINGLET: *(returning)* Nothing, I looked everywhere. What's happened to the hat?!

PAILLARDIN: My nightshirt and my slippers. He's stolen my shirt and my slippers. A pajama thief.

PINGLET: Marcelle's going to make a scene. What can I do? I'll have to tell her the truth.

PAILLARDIN: I'll have to sleep in my clothes. If anything happens I'll be ready for action. *(on bed)*

(Pinglet enters room 10)

MARCELLE: You're back finally. Well, where's my hat?

PINGLET: Marcelle, be brave.

MARCELLE: Why?

PINGLET: I can't find it. Someone's taken it.

MARCELLE: Who?

PINGLET: He didn't leave his name.

MARCELLE: Oh, charming. Luckily I have my lace scarf. I'll wear that. We must leave immediately.

PINGLET: We're going. I've had enough.

MARCELLE: *You've* had enough? I've learned my lesson. And what a lesson.

PAILLARDIN: I'm really tired. Can't keep my eyes open. *(yawns)* Don't know what's the matter with me ... sleep!

(Marcelle and Pinglet are leaving the lobby)

MARCELLE: Oh, my God, it's Maxime.

PINGLET: With Victoire. Disgusting! What's the world coming to?

MARCELLE: Shut the door!

PINGLET: The key? Where's the key? I don't have the key.

MARCELLE: It doesn't matter! Shut the door!

PINGLET: But I can't lock it. Get in there *(gesturing toward the toilet)*. We can bolt the door. Come on!

MARCELLE: What a night. What a night.

(Victoire and Maxime enter with books and satchel)

BASTIEN: This way, sir, welcome to the Paradise Hotel.

MAXIME: This is a very serious step we are taking, mademoiselle.

VICTOIRE: *(smiling)* Why don't you drop it! A serious step!

BASTIEN: I know just what Monsieur and Madame are looking for. A little love nest away from home, where love can blossom and no questions asked. And your madame is very beautiful too, sir. Very beautiful.

MAXIME: Yes, oh, thank you! Do you really think so?

BASTIEN: Oh, you are in luck tonight, number 9 is available. This was the room in which his Royal Highness the Grand Prince of Poland spent his honeymoon night ... with his chambermaid.

VICTOIRE: The royal suite!

BASTIEN: This is a truly first-class establishment.

VICTOIRE: Yes, I know. We read the brochure. Good, well then, we'll take number 9.

BASTIEN: Excellent choice, madame, excellent choice. *(he grins)*

MAXIME: Mademoiselle, he's laughing at me. Even the porter's laughing at me.

VICTOIRE: Oh, let him laugh.

BASTIEN: *(with candle)* If you'd like to follow me please? *(Victoire is pulling Maxime)*

MAXIME: Mademoiselle, wait a minute. I don't know where this will end up.

VICTOIRE: I do. Trust me.

MAXIME: I think I'm ready. I'm glad I read my Descartes.

VICTOIRE: I'll give you some Spinoza. *(they go upstairs)*

(Paillardin is sleeping, the girls enter)

VIOLET: Time for bed. Well, I'm ready. *(they scramble to get beds)*

MARGARITE: I've got dibs on this one.

PERVENCHE: I've got dibs on this one.

PAQUERETTE: No, that's mine.

79

PERVENCHE: No, it isn't.

(improvised fight) e.g. Yes it is. No. I saw it first. Didn't. Did. Didn't. Did. etc....

VIOLET: Not so much noise. Remember what papa said. Oh, I can't wait to get between the sheets. *(gets in)* Brrrr, it's freezing.

PERVENCHE: Oh dear, I should put my hair in curlers before I go to sleep.

PAQUERETTE: Me too.

MARGARITE: Yes.

VIOLET: Let's do our hair. What are you doing? Come on.

BASTIEN: *(upstairs)* Good night, sir. Good night, madame.

PERVENCHE: Pass me the candle.

MARGARITE: Give it to me.

PERVENCHE: No, me.

ALL: Me, me, etc.... *(candle goes out)*

VIOLET: Now you've done it.

MARGARITE: Let's light our night lights. *(little blue lights)*

VIOLET: Look, look at us. We look like little elves.

PERVENCHE: *(on her bed)* Yes, we look like ghosts.

VIOLET: It's true. I'm the headless ghost of the Paradise Hotel. Ooooooh.

(Violet starts to sing, they all join in)

Come out, come out,
Wherever you are,

Out of the cold, cold ground.
So, wake up ghosts,
Wherever you are,
We're dancing round and round.

PAILLARDIN: Ghosts! Oh, my God!

ALL: Come out, come out,
Wherever you are,
Out of the cold, cold ground.
So, wake up ghosts,
Wherever you are,
We're dancing round and round.

PAILLARDIN: *(standing on his bed)* Get thee behind me Satan!

ALL: Aaaugh. *(run to toilet)*

PAILLARDIN: Ghosts, it's the ghosts. Help! Help!

VICTOIRE AND MAXIME: *(they come out in their underwear)* What's going on?

PAILLARDIN: Help! Help! *(races past them without seeing them)*

VICTOIRE: Monsieur Paillardin! *(she hides behind the curtains of Mathieu's bed)*

MAXIME: My uncle. *(runs into his own room)*

PAILLARDIN: Ghosts! Bogeys! Spirits! *(exits)*

MATHIEU: *(entering)* What are you going on about? A man? Where? There's no man. A man in the bed? *(opens curtains)* Oh, sorry.

VICTOIRE: Oh.

MATHIEU: Oh, I beg your pardon, madame. *(aside)* They call that a man? That's a woman. *(back to bathroom)* That's not a man, that's a woman.

81

GIRLS: Honestly, Papa, there was a man. There really was.

MAXIME: My uncle must have gone. I'd better see what's happened to Victoire. *(enters)* No one here. Victoire!

VICTOIRE: Monsieur Maxime, over here. *(she opens the curtains)*

MATHIEU: All right, girls, come in and see for yourselves.

MAXIME AND VICTOIRE: Oh *(they hide)*.

VIOLET: Honestly, Papa, there was a man. We saw him.

MATHIEU: Me too, I had a good look. It would be terrible if I couldn't tell a man from a woman, especially at my age. See, *(Victoire is creeping out)* I knew what I was talking about. That's definitely a woman. That is a woman! *(Maxime is crawling out)*

GIRLS: No, Papa, look, it's a man.

MATHIEU: A man and a woman? *(They face each other. Maxime and Victoire exit hastily.)*

MAXIME: I've had enough of this hotel. Let's go.

VICTOIRE: How about the Continental?

MATHIEU: We've got to get to the bottom of this. Boy! Porter!

BOULOT: What's the matter? What's all the noise about?

MATHIEU: Now what have you got to say about this.... We have found ... in our room ... men and women. Both kinds.

BOULOT: What, sir? Really? Well, sir, you see ... er ...

MATHIEU: What!

BOULOT: I hate to tell you this, sir, but that room is haunted.

ALL: Haunted?

(Paillardin is creeping down the stairs)

BOULOT: Yes, sir, what you thought were ... both kinds ... they were really ghosts, sir.

GIRLS: Ghosts! Aaaaaaah. *(they run past Paillardin who is terrified and runs away again)*

MATHIEU: Girls, girls, you can't run around in your nightgowns. Girls!

BOULOT: My God, what a mess! What a mess!

(Pinglet and Marcelle enter from the bathroom)

PINGLET: What's all the commotion about? All that shouting.

MARCELLE: I tell you there's something strange going on in this hotel. I'm scared to death. Please, let's get out of here.

PINGLET: Yes, of course. But wait a minute. Got to be careful! *(opens door)*

MARCELLE: I won't feel at peace until I'm out of this place.

PINGLET: No one. Come!

MARCELLE: At last.

PAILLARDIN: *(returning)* My God, ghosts, ghosts!

MARCELLE: Oh my God, get back!

PINGLET: What is it?

MARCELLE: My husband.

PINGLET: Ah. *(shuts door)*

PAILLARDIN: Thank God! Real live human beings! *(tries to open door)* Open the door! Please! Let me in. *(pushes hard)*

PINGLET: This room is reserved.

PAILLARDIN: Let me in. For the love of God!

MARCELLE: Don't open it.

PINGLET: I don't think I can keep it closed. He has the strength of a madman.

PAILLARDIN: Open up! *(Pushes door so hard Pinglet goes up chimney. Marcelle grabs Paillardin's hat, puts it on.)*

PAILLARDIN: That's my hat! Madame, my hat. *(tries to take it)*

MARCELLE: *(shouts)* Help! Help!

(Pinglet emerges in black face)

PAILLARDIN: The chimney sweep? *(Pinglet hits him in the eye)* Oh! the ghosts are back. *(Pinglet kicks him)* Ghosts that go bump in the night. *(he runs away)*

PINGLET: Marcelle, Marcelle, he's gone.

MARCELLE: At last. My God, what a nightmare! *(sees him)* My God, a Zulu.

PINGLET: It's me, Pinglet.

MARCELLE: Oh, Pinglet. This night will be the death of me. You've changed color.

PINGLET: Yes, yes. That doesn't matter.

MARCELLE: My God, when I think what we've been through. The terror, the emotions.

PINGLET: It's all over now, thank goodness. We can take a deep breath.

MARCELLE: Yes, thank heavens for that. What a relief.

PINGLET: Yes, feels good, feels good. *(shouts are heard)* What's that?

MARCELLE: Not again!

BASTIEN: *(running into lobby)* Oh, my God, it's the police! The police! Beat it! Quick, it's the vice squad!

PINGLET: The vice squad?

BASTIEN: The vice squad.

MARCELLE: What does he mean?

PINGLET: The vice squad! The police. We're done for, it's the police.

MARCELLE: The police? We must get out of here. *(sees Boucard and other police)* Aaaaah ... a police inspector! *(shuts door)*

BOUCARD: There's one now. *(sees Pinglet)* Arrest that man!

PINGLET: Me? Now look here, I have my rights.

A COP: Yeah, yeah, later.

BOUCARD: Open that door.

MARCELLE: You can't come in. This room is reserved.

BOUCARD: Force it open!

MARCELLE: It's all over.

COP: Come with me.

PINGLET: The poor woman.

MARCELLE: My God!

BOUCARD: Over here, madame.

MARCELLE: What do you want with me? I'm an honest woman.

PINGLET: Yes, sir! That lady is an honest woman.

BOUCARD: Good for her. No one asked you anyway. Take him in there.

PINGLET: *(resisting)* Now hold on, hold on a minute. *(he is taken into room 22)*

COP: Move it. No more lip.

BOUCARD: Now it's your turn, madame, and I don't want no horse feathers. Name and address, please.

MARCELLE: I don't understand what this is all about. I'm here with my husband.

BOUCARD: Your husband? Bull. . . .

MARCELLE: Yes, my husband. I am the wife of . . . the man you just took in there.

BOUCARD: Sure, sure. I could tell. Would it be indiscreet to ask your name? *(pronounced* nim)

MARCELLE: Name?

BOUCARD: Inspector Bouc—Nim?!

MARCELLE: But monsieur, I . . . *(aside)* What else can I do? My name is . . . Madame Pinglet.

BOUCARD: Very good. Bring him in, will you?

COP: Out here, you.

PINGLET: My God, the poor woman. She's probably given her real name.

BOUCARD: And you, sir, what's your nim?

PINGLET: What?

BOUCHARD: Nim.

PINGLET: I don't quite understand ... my behavior is above reproach, and that lady is my wife.

MARCELLE: *(gleam of hope)* Ah.

BOUCARD: *(aside)* Maybe I was wrong. And your name, sir?

PINGLET: Madame, I'm sure has already told you, Monsieur Paillardin.

MARCELLE: Oh, my God.

BOUCARD: Thank you very much, sir. It's just as I thought.

MARCELLE: I'm ruined.

PINGLET: I saved her.

BOUCARD: Take them all in. Lock them up.

ACT 3

Pinglet's office. Early next morning. Pinglet enters, in black face, through the window. He crosses to the door and finds that it is still locked. He goes into the bedroom, puts on a dressing gown, and accidentally finds the key in his pocket.

PINGLET: Good. I look as if I just got up. She can come home anytime she likes. She won't know a thing! What a night. My God, what a night! *(knock)* It's her. She's early. No, she's got the key, she wouldn't knock. Who is it?

VICTOIRE: It's me, sir, Victoire.

PINGLET: *(aside)* Victoire, slut. Another customer of the Paradise Hotel, but I can't say a word to her without giving myself away. What do you want?

VICTOIRE: Your hot chocolate, sir.

PINGLET: Oh good, come in.

VICTOIRE: I can't, I haven't got a key, sir.

PINGLET: *(taking out his key)* Don't I know it.... Well, go and ask Madame Pinglet for it. She's got it.

VICTOIRE: But she hasn't come back yet, sir.

PINGLET: Really? Her sister must have taken a turn for the worse. *(aside)* Well, with my wife there I'm not surprised.

89

VICTOIRE: What do you want me to do, sir?

PINGLET: I don't know. I don't have the key. We'll wait for my wife to get back.

VICTOIRE: Yes, sir.

PINGLET: I'm not so dumb. I could have opened it, but then ... bye-bye alibi. Oooh what a night. Arrested like a pair of crooks, common thieves, just because Marcelle and I ... and we didn't even get to do it. *(knock)* Who is it?

MARCELLE: Pinglet, it's me.

PINGLET: Who's me?

MARCELLE: Me!! Marcelle.

PINGLET: Are you alone?

MARCELLE: Yes, open up.

PINGLET: Wait a second. Pull the bolt on your side.

MARCELLE: There we go.

PINGLET: Quick, come in. *(locks door)* Oh, Marcelle, what a night! My God, what a night!

MARCELLE: Oh, Pinglet, you have ruined me.

PINGLET: No, I haven't. Not at all. It's not that serious. We were caught in a hotel together— what's wrong with that? We're not criminals. When the police raid a place they're looking for criminals, crooks.

MARCELLE: But the police ... once they get their hands on you they're all over you.

PINGLET: My God, what happened?

MARCELLE: No no. Papers. Forms. And if my

90

husband ... oh, if he found anything ... it would be all over. Pinglet, what's to become of me?

PINGLET: *(kneels, kisses her)* Come on, be brave, come on. You mustn't be a scaredy-cat. What's that on your face? It's dirty.

MARCELLE: Dirty? Me? No, you put it there. Go look at your face.

(He goes to the mirror. She dips a napkin in the water glass from last night's dinner. He wipes his face clean.)

PINGLET: Damnation, it's from last night, that chimney. Lucky my wife didn't see it. "Sure! I was home all night." One thing after another.

MARCELLE: What a night. My God, what a night!

PINGLET: You're right. Terrible night. But it might have been worse. We could have spent it in jail with all the others. But thank God the inspector trusted us and I was able to post bail.

MARCELLE: Of course he could see at once the class of person he was dealing with.

PINGLET: You're right there. Of course, the five thousand francs I slipped him came in handy, too. Is it all off?

MARCELLE: There's just a spot on the tip. *(hits him with napkin)* Five thousand francs? You slipped him five thousand francs?

PINGLET: Yes, I gave him a choice: he could take my word as a gentleman or the five thousand francs. He took the money and this afternoon all I have to do is prove that we are who we said we were.

MARCELLE: Pinglet, how can you prove that you are Monsieur Paillardin? You can't. They'll be round here like a shot.

91

PINGLET: No, they won't come here. I know what to do. This morning I'm going to the chief of police.

MARCELLE: The chief of police?

PINGLET: Yes. Last night while you were sleeping peacefully in your little bed ...

MARCELLE: Peacefully? What do you mean peacefully?

PINGLET: All right, not peacefully. Do you know where I was? I was at the house of the chief of police.

MARCELLE: What did he say?

PINGLET: He was out. Dancing. But I waited there until seven o'clock this morning.

MARCELLE: What did he say?

PINGLET: Good morning! Then he went straight to bed. Doesn't matter, I'll go back. He and I are like this. *(crosses his fingers)*

MARCELLE: Really?

PINGLET: I'll tell him everything.

MARCELLE: Don't be a fool.

PINGLET: I'll tell him this is a question of a woman's honor. He'll take care of it.

MARCELLE: You're sure?

PINGLET: We're like this. *(crosses his fingers)*

MARCELLE: We could have avoided this whole thing. Why on earth did you say that you were Monsieur Paillardin? Everyone knows you're Monsieur Pinglet.

PINGLET: Me? It was you. Why on earth did you say

that you were Madame Pinglet? Everyone knows you're Madame Paillardin.

MARCELLE: Excuse me, I said my name was Madame Pinglet so they'd think I was your wife.

PINGLET: Excuse me, I said my name was Paillardin so they'd think I was your husband.

MARCELLE: Yes, but come on, sweetheart, you don't expect the police inspector to believe that your wife's name is Pinglet when your name is Paillardin.

PINGLET: Now look here, sweetie, how could I guess that when I said my name was Paillardin, you'd already said yours was Pinglet?

MARCELLE: When your brain is empty you should keep your mouth shut.

PINGLET: *(aside)* Women! *(knock)* Who's there?

PAILLARDIN: It's me, Paillardin.

MARCELLE: My husband!

PINGLET: Shhhh! What is it you want?

PAILLARDIN: I need to speak to you.

PINGLET: I can't open the door. My wife locked me in and took the key.

PAILLARDIN: Damnation!

PINGLET: Wait a second, I know. Go outside, get the gardener's ladder, and climb through the window.

PAILLARDIN: Great idea! Good. But aren't you ashamed of yourself—letting your wife do that to you?

PINGLET: That's life, what are you going to do?

PAILLARDIN: If my wife ever did that to me . . . but of

course she wouldn't try it because she knows what she would get.

MARCELLE: *(starts to speak)* You—! ...

PINGLET: Can go now.

PAILLARDIN: I'm off to get the ladder.

PINGLET: Good.

MARCELLE: Now, open the door.

PINGLET: Wait, I can still hear his footsteps ... you can go now.

MARCELLE: All right, all right.

PINGLET: Bolt the door after you.

MARCELLE: What a night. My God, what a night! *(exits)*

PINGLET: Yes, what a night, my God what a night! *(crosses to window)* ... Are you all right?

PAILLARDIN: I'm coming up.

PINGLET: Steady on, careful.

PAILLARDIN: There we go. *(entering)* Oh, what a night. My God, what a night! *(Paillardin has a black eye)*

PINGLET: What's the matter with your eye?

PAILLARDIN: Oh, have I been through the wringer! Do you believe in ghosts?

PINGLET: Of course not.

PAILLARDIN: I was the same way, but I tell you my friend ... we must believe. I've seen them with my own two eyes.

PINGLET: You have?

94

PAILLARDIN: I've seen them, I tell you. Face to face.

PINGLET: You've seen ghosts. *(laugh)* Of course you have. Booooo!

PAILLARDIN: I have, I tell you. I didn't believe in them. I was like you. When I went to the hotel it was just a big joke. You know, I said it was the pipes, the drains—not true! I had been asleep for perhaps half an hour in a room they said was haunted, right? I woke up, right? Little pale creatures like elves, or something, dancing in a circle, wispy little voices, flickering lights all around me, and they were singing ... or maybe chanting. Yes, go on, laugh, but I was *there* and I'll never forget it!
    Come out, come out,
    Wherever you are,
    Out of the cold, cold ground.
    So, wake up ghosts,
    Wherever you are,
    We're dancing round and round.
—scared the hell out of me.

PINGLET: *(aside)* With a voice like that, I'm not surprised!

PAILLARDIN: I didn't have time to say goodbye, let me tell you. Out! I grabbed this and that and I was gone. Like a bat out of hell. Then what do I see? ... in a room across the way I see two people ... living human beings ... that room, oh, that room.

PINGLET: Room 10.

PAILLARDIN: Room 10. I don't know. Why Room 10?

PINGLET: I don't know, why not Room 10?

PAILLARDIN: All right, Room 10. I moved towards it, what do I see?

PINGLET: What?

PAILLARDIN: I see a woman, or something that looked like a woman, with this dress on and these ... and, you know ... but I couldn't see her face. She was wearing my hat.

PINGLET: Your hat?

PAILLARDIN: Yes, I don't know how, I couldn't take it all in, but ... that dress, oh, that dress, I'll never forget it.

PINGLET: Damnation!

PAILLARDIN: It was a sort of puce color and had these ... things hanging down from it. And then ...

PINGLET: What?

PAILLARDIN: ... I'm, I'm telling you. This was real magic, black magic. Out comes a chimney sweep. Why? How? Where? I don't know. A chimney sweep—about your size as a matter of fact.

PINGLET: I'd say he was smaller.

PAILLARDIN: What do you mean, smaller?

PINGLET: Chimney sweeps are always much smaller— it's the size of the hole, basically.

PAILLARDIN: You may be right. I didn't have time for a tape measure. Anyway, before I knew what was happening, *pow*, he hit me! And then he kicked me right in the ... that's the last time I'm going there, I can tell you! Paradise Hotel, it was the hotel from hell. Devils! Ghosts! Poltergeists!

PINGLET: *(aside)* He believes it! He believes that we were ghosts. Tell me, what does your wife think of your ghost stories?

PAILLARDIN: My wife—I haven't seen her yet. When I came back last night I knocked and knocked but she didn't answer the door.

PINGLET: Damnation.

PAILLARDIN: Sleeping like a log, so I had to sleep in the guest room.

MAXIME: *(from the garden)* Uncle! Uncle!

PAILLARDIN: Good Lord! That sounds like Maxime.

PINGLET: Yes, it does.

PAILLARDIN: What are you doing *here*. Why aren't you at the college.

MAXIME: I can explain.

PAILLARDIN: You'll have to come up the ladder.

MAXIME: I'm coming.

PAILLARDIN: He'd better explain!

MAXIME: *(enters through window, cigarette in mouth)* Morning, Monsieur Pinglet. Morning, Uncle. That's a beauty. What happened?

PAILLARDIN: Nothing, nothing. You look wide awake. Why aren't you at school?

MAXIME: Well, I was just about to tell you. It's very strange. I don't know how it happened.... I forgot to wind my watch in the morning and last night, when I got to the college, all the gates were locked.

PAILLARDIN: Now, what are you trying to say? Is this some kind of a joke?

MAXIME: Uncle, a joke? I'm a very serious person, Uncle.

97

PINGLET: *(aside)* Not a bad performance.

PAILLARDIN: So why didn't you come back here right away?

MAXIME: Because it was much too late, Uncle. And I knew that you wouldn't be here, and I didn't want to disturb Aunt Marcelle.

PAILLARDIN: So ... where did you spend the night, boy?

MAXIME: At the Continental, Uncle. Nice place.

PAILLARDIN: True?

MAXIME: Absolutely, sir.

PINGLET: *(aside)* He lies through his teeth, this philosopher.

MAXIME: And when I got to the college this morning, the house master said he needed a letter from you.

PAILLARDIN: All right, we'll see.

MAXIME: Thank God—he didn't recognize me.

MARCELLE: *(knock)* Henri! Henri!

PAILLARDIN: That sounds like my wife. I'm in here, sweetheart.

MARCELLE: So, open the door.

PAILLARDIN: I can't. It's locked. Madame Pinglet has the key. I had to climb in through the window. I'm with Pinglet.

MARCELLE: I see.

PINGLET: Morning, madame!

MARCELLE: Good morning, Monsieur Pinglet.

PINGLET: *(as though he could see her)* And how are you this morning? Sleep well?

MARCELLE: Oh, so so. I had a restless night.

PINGLET: Well, it's a new day, isn't it?

PAILLARDIN: Talking of restless nights ... *I* had a restless night you wouldn't believe. You know what happened to me?

MARCELLE: No. What?

PAILLARDIN: It was beyond belief. You know the Paradise Hotel?

MARCELLE: Of course I don't. Of course I don't.

PINGLET: No, of course we don't. Of course we don't.

MAXIME: Nor me. Nor me.

PAILLARDIN: I know you don't know it. It's a ... well, it's a disreputable place. How would you know it?

PINGLET, MAXIME, AND MARCELLE: Of course. Quite right. Of course.

PAILLARDIN: Anyway. Back to the hotel. But damn it, I can't talk through the door. I'll pop out of the window, through the garden—be with you in a minute.

MARCELLE: All right.

PAILLARDIN: Do you mind? We parted on pretty poor terms last night. I'd like to make it up to her.

PINGLET: Of course.

PAILLARDIN: *(to Maxime)* Get out of the way! Go on,

I'll follow you down. Are you coming down? *(they exit through the window)*

PINGLET: Not me, no no. I'll stay here, right here. *(aside)* Thank you, got to keep my alibi. Oh, take the ladder away. Put it away for me. *(Pinglet opens the door)*

MARCELLE: Has my husband gone?

PINGLET: Yes.

MARCELLE: What did he tell you?

PINGLET: Nothing. He knows nothing. Everything's fine. He doesn't suspect a thing.

MARCELLE: Oh, thank God.

PINGLET: Holy—! There's one thing—the dress you wore last night. That's all he saw. The only clue. Tear it up. Burn it. Give it away. But for the love of God, don't let him set eyes on it!

MARCELLE: Thank heavens you told me. I'll get rid of it right away. *(she exits)*

PINGLET: Quick, off you go. Bolt the door. All right, everything's fine. Calm down. But I'm beginning to feel like a fool stuck in here. I hope to God Angelique comes back soon. I know her sister's sick, but this is ridiculous. What about me?

VICTOIRE: *(offstage)* Sir, sir.

PINGLET: Is that you, Victoire?

VICTOIRE: *(she enters through the window, a telegram on the salver)* A telegram for you, sir.

PINGLET: Probably from my wife. You can go back down now.

VICTOIRE: Yes, sir.

PINGLET: Put the ladder away. No, it's from her sister. "Very worried. Angelique not here for dinner. Waited until midnight." Midnight, she says! "Is she ill? Please telegraph!" What's going on? My wife wasn't with her sister. Let me think. Now last night she left for ... *(smiles)* perhaps she's been kidnaped. No. These days, acts of heroism are very rare. Wait a minute, wait a minute, perhaps Madame Pinglet has been up to a little hanky-panky, a blind date perhaps? Well, he'd have to be, wouldn't he?

ANGELIQUE: *(offstage)* Pinglet, Pinglet!

PINGLET: That's her.

ANGELIQUE: Pinglet!

PINGLET: She sounds a bit shaky. *(yawns)* Time to get out of bed. *(goes to his room)*

ANGELIQUE: Ah, Pinglet, my dear sweet, adorable Pinglet. *(enters with big black eye)* What a night. My God, what a night! Benoit, Benoit, where are you?

PINGLET: Who's that, who's there.

ANGELIQUE: It's me. Oh Lord Almighty. Where are you? I'm still alive.

PINGLET: Good.

ANGELIQUE: Oh, my God! When he finds out what happened to me—the utter disaster I've been through, and he's been sleeping peacefully in his little bed. Benoit.

PINGLET: *(enters)* Here I am.

ANGELIQUE: Oh Benoit, I'm so happy to see you. *(crosses to him)*

101

PINGLET: Me too, but why?

ANGELIQUE: Oh Benoit, what a night, my God, what a night!

PINGLET: Where have I heard that before? Oh, but look at me, what's happened? Ooh la la, you've got a terrible black eye.

ANGELIQUE: Oh Pinglet, Pinglet, I can tell you now. You almost lost me.

PINGLET: How close?

ANGELIQUE: Very.

PINGLET: Oh.

ANGELIQUE: Does that upset you?

PINGLET: Of course.

ANGELIQUE: Oh, my love. An accident, a terrible accident which almost, almost took me from you.

PINGLET: Don't keep on about it. You're breaking my heart.

ANGELIQUE: You're such a good husband. I took a cab, as you know, to go to Ville d'Avray. At first, everything was fine. We were having a very nice time, the three of us.

PINGLET: Three of you?

ANGELIQUE: Yes, me, the driver and the horse. But when suddenly, well! A train let off this piercing whistle—we were right by the gates of Paris and the horse bolted and I almost ...

PINGLET: Don't tell me.

ANGELIQUE: ... yes ... almost. The driver tried to hold him back. No use. There we were—hurtling,

102

flying through space, the horse galloping out of control. Not a soul in sight. It's at moments like this that one knows what it means to love one's husband. You understand. Here I was, hurtling along, no chance of escape, Death staring me in the face, and all I could think of was—I wish he were here.

PINGLET: Well, thanks a lot, nice of you to think of me.

ANGELIQUE: But tragically, you weren't there to help.

PINGLET: A shame, really.

ANGELIQUE: So, all alone, I just lost my head. I opened the door of the carriage, closed my eyes, and jumped.

PINGLET: *(very calm)* Good God!

ANGELIQUE: And, kerplop! Head first into ... into ... a pile of ... of ...

PINGLET: You poor thing.

ANGELIQUE: After that, I don't remember anything. All I know is that in the morning, I woke up in a hut. A peasant's cottage with all these faces, country faces, looking down on me. Grinning. I think they were happy to see me alive.

PINGLET: Maybe.

ANGELIQUE: They were so good to me. I wish I'd had a hundred francs with me. They saved my life. I'd have given it all to them.

PINGLET: That might have been overly generous.

ANGELIQUE: But they saved my life!

PINGLET: *(aside)* That's what I meant.

ANGELIQUE: What?

PINGLET: Heaven sent.

ANGELIQUE: Finally, later this morning, when they saw I was getting better, they put me on a sort of vegetable cart—rutabagas, I think they were—and took me as far as the Champs Elysees. From there I got a cab, and here I am!

PINGLET: Tragic.

ANGELIQUE: Oh, Pinglet, when I think of it, when I remember that split second in the air, *(mimes)* your poor little wife . . .

PINGLET: There, there, don't cry, it's all over.

ANGELIQUE: But what if you'd lost me, what would you have done?

PINGLET: *(holding her)* I'll tell you honestly, I'd never marry again.

VICTOIRE: *(enters)* Madame, the mail is here.

ANGELIQUE: Put it down over there.

PINGLET: I'm going to get dressed. *(exits)*

ANGELIQUE: All right. Ooh la la, I feel a bit dizzy. I need a nice warm bath.

VICTOIRE: Oh, what's happened, madame? Perhaps you hadn't noticed, you've got this great big black eye.

ANGELIQUE: Hadn't noticed? I often wonder how you got this job. Yes, I've noticed. Off you go, and prepare my bath.

VICTOIRE: Yes, madame.

ANGELIQUE: Put some milk in the bath.

VICTOIRE: Yes, ma'am. Oh, the cat drank all the milk this morning.

ANGELIQUE: What else have you got?

VICTOIRE: Some herring.

ANGELIQUE: For the bath, not the cat!

VICTOIRE: Some baking soda?

ANGELIQUE: That will do.

VICTOIRE: Yes, ma'am.

ANGELIQUE: *(picking up letters)* What have we got ...

PINGLET: *(singing)* Through the tulips with my love....

ANGELIQUE: What's all this? "Police Inspector Boucard." What do they want with me? "You are hereby summoned to appear at my office to answer certain charges and to bring your identification papers." What does this mean? "To Madame Pinglet, who was arrested last night in the company of Monsieur Paillardin"—what?!—"in the police raid on the Paradise Hotel." Arres ...uh ...Mon ...a raa ...by the poo ...this is ... absurd. Absurd, absurd. There must be some mistake. *(touching her head)* Am I hallucinating?

PINGLET: *(enters with boot in hand and rings bell)* There's a button missing off my boot.

ANGELIQUE: Thank God, you're here!

PINGLET: What's the matter now?

ANGELIQUE: I think I may be going mad. I think I've forgotten how to read. It says ... it says ... oh, it's too awful! You read it.

PINGLET: Damn it! The police already.

ANGELIQUE: Read it. Read it.

PINGLET: We're done for—the two of us. "To Madame Pinglet, who was arrested last night in the company of Monsieur Paillardin in the police raid on the Paradise Hotel."

ANGELIQUE: That's me, me! I was arrested last night in the company of Monsieur Paillardin.

PINGLET: *(turning on her)* You hussy! You admit it!

ANGELIQUE: What?

PINGLET: You were arrested? You? And with Paillardin! *(hits the table with his boot)*

ANGELIQUE: Oh, no, he believes it!.... No, no.

PINGLET: Back, woman.

ANGELIQUE: Pinglet!

PINGLET: And what were you doing with Paillardin? Huh?? What were you doing?

ANGELIQUE: Nothing, I swear to you, it's all absurd, quite absurd.

PINGLET: This letter has got a stamp on it. It's official. What were you doing? Confess, it's all over. *(shakes her by the wrist)*

ANGELIQUE: You're hurting me, you're hurting me.

PINGLET: Confess!

ANGELIQUE: I can't confess to something that's not true.

PINGLET: *(raising boot)* Take that!

ANGELIQUE: *(on floor)* Aaaaah!

VICTOIRE: *(enters)* Did you ring, sir?

PINGLET: Yes, I'm missing a button off this boot. Here we are. Make sure it stays on.

VICTOIRE: Yes, sir. *(aside)* What's going on?

PINGLET: *(turning back)* You Clytemnestra, you. You Jezebel! There she is, the woman I trusted—I believed in. I always said to my friends ... "All right," I'd say, "maybe she is a battle axe and boring to live with, but she's faithful." But now ... you Delilah, you, and at your age!

ANGELIQUE: But it's not true, I tell you, it's not true. *(follows him around on her knees)*

PINGLET: I see it all now. That's why you locked me up in here. So you could play your games of lust and sin, with Paillardin, my best friend. Playing doctor with an architect!

ANGELIQUE: No! Never!

PINGLET: And where did you spend the night? In the Paradise Hotel! A filthy little hotel on the rue de Provence.

ANGELIQUE: It's just not true. Never! I didn't even know it was in the rue de Provence. Who told you it was in the rue de Provence.

PINGLET: It says so right here. *(takes letter)* Oh, no, it doesn't.

ANGELIQUE: You see, I'm telling the truth—the horse and the peasants ... they looked after me.

PINGLET: Where were they, those peasants?

ANGELIQUE: In their village.

PINGLET: And where is that village?

ANGELIQUE: My God, I'm telling you the truth, I don't remember. It was far away, I was dizzy, and ... I should have asked them ... but the shock. Paillardin!

PINGLET: Ah ha!

ANGELIQUE: No, he's accused too. So he can tell you. He'll show you it's not true.

PINGLET: We'll see about that. *(at window)* Speak of the devil. He's just crossing the garden. Paillardin! Paillardin!

PAILLARDIN: What?

PINGLET: Come up here. I want to talk to you.

PAILLARDIN: What do you want to talk about?

PINGLET: Come up and you'll find out.

ANGELIQUE: You'll be sorry....

PINGLET: And you, madame. Not a word! Not a nod or a wink—no signals to your partner in sin. Silence in court.

ANGELIQUE: My God! My God, you who know everything and see everything, look down upon this innocent lamb.

PAILLARDIN: Well, what is it?

PINGLET: Step over here please, sir.

PAILLARDIN: Sir? What's the matter?

ANGELIQUE: Ah, Paillardin ...

PINGLET: Madame, not a word. Let justice prevail. Where did you say you spent last night?

PAILLARDIN: The Paradise Hotel.

ANGELIQUE: Oh oh oh.

PAILLARDIN: 220 rue de Provence.

PINGLET: You hear that, madame?

ANGELIQUE: My God, I'm going out of my mind. It can't be true! It can't be. With ... ? Oh no.

PAILLARDIN: What is the matter with them?

PINGLET: And who was with you at this Paradise Hotel? Who was with you?

PAILLARDIN: I was alone.

PINGLET: The truth. I want the truth! You were with my wife.

PAILLARDIN: What?

PINGLET: The game's up, Paillardin. You are my wife's lover.

PAILLARDIN: Me? Don't be rid—

ANGELIQUE: You see? I told yo—

PINGLET: Silence in court.

PAILLARDIN: Oh, come on, stop it. You've had your little joke.

PINGLET: Joke? Read that. You call that a joke?

PAILLARDIN: What's all this? "To Madame Pinglet who was arrested last night in the company of Monsieur Paillardin in the police raid on the Paradise Hotel." That's funny! This is a farce, I mean a real farce!

PINGLET: A farce, eh. Do I look as if I think it's funny?

ANGELIQUE: My husband thinks that I could ... I mean, that I did ... with you ... yes, honestly.

PAILLARDIN: Me? With you? Your lover? That's funny, that's really funny!

PINGLET: I think you'd better stop laughing.

PAILLARDIN: But you can't be serious. You really think I would? But that's stupid of you.... I mean, you're being really stupid.

PINGLET: Insults will get you nowhere.

(Angelique throws herself on the sofa)

PAILLARDIN: But me? The lover of ... *(sotto voce)* Listen here, we're old friends, and I don't want to be rude or impolite, but take a look at her—seriously, before you start accusing me.... Please, I mean, just look at her!

PINGLET: This is no time to insult my wife.

ANGELIQUE: Is he insulting me?

PINGLET: Yes, madame, that's exactly what he's doing. He put you on a pedestal like a goddess, and now he's knocking you off it. He'll toss you aside like a squeezed-out lemon.

PAILLARDIN: You really are stupid.

PINGLET: Sticks and stones. But how do you explain that?

PAILLARDIN: I don't know, someone's got a bizarre sense of humor. It's obvious. Look, if I was implicated with your wife in this so-called raid, why haven't I received a summons, too? But I've received nothing—you hear me? Nothing! And until I do, I'll deny, deny, deny till my last breath.

VICTOIRE: *(crosses to Paillardin)* Sir, there's a letter for Monsieur Paillardin from the Chief of Police.

PAILLARDIN: "To Monsieur Paillardin, who was arrested last night in the company of Madame Pinglet in the police raid on the Paradise Hotel."

PINGLET: Ah ha. That's got you.

PAILLARDIN: This is too much.

ANGELIQUE: Fate has us in its grasp.

PINGLET: Deny deny deny.

PAILLARDIN: I don't understand. I'm going out of my mind.

VICTOIRE: Sir, your boot.

PINGLET: Thanks a lot. *(to Paillardin)* Oh you traitor, you double-dyed traitor.

VICTOIRE: Sorry, sir.

PINGLET: Not you, go away.

VICTOIRE: Yes, sir.

(Marcelle enters)

PAILLARDIN: Marcelle.

PINGLET: Ah, Madame Paillardin. Just in time ... you see this man?

MARCELLE: It's my husband.

PINGLET: Yes, him. He, madame, is my wife's lover.

MARCELLE: He is?

PAILLARDIN AND ANGELIQUE: Oh, my God!

PINGLET: *(aside)* It's not true. Just faint, quick, into my arms.

MARCELLE: Right. Ahhhhh.

PAILLARDIN: It's a lie, it's a lie! Oh, my God! You must be mad to tell her that. Marcelle, Marcelle. Smelling salts, quick!

ANGELIQUE: Here, I've got some in here.
(they leave)

MARCELLE: What's going on?

PINGLET: They both got summonses. So to get us off the hook, I told them ... you got it?

MARCELLE: I got it. *(they re-enter)*

PINGLET: Faint again.

PAILLARDIN: The salts. *(using the flask like a revolver and pointing at Pinglet)* What you have done, sir, is unworthy of a gentleman.

PINGLET: And you, sir, had better come off your high horse. Don't stuff it up her nose like that. It'll burn a hole. Give it here.

PAILLARDIN: Oh, my God! What a tragedy. Water, I need some water.

PINGLET: *(to Marcelle)* That's enough. You can wake up now.

MARCELLE: Right. Ahhhhhh.

ANGELIQUE: She's coming to.

PAILLARDIN: Marcelle, Marcelle, please! I beg you! Don't believe a word he said.

ANGELIQUE: It's lies, all lies.

PINGLET: They were caught. Together. Last night in a raid by the police.

MARCELLE: That's terrible. *(to Pinglet)* Shall I faint?

PINGLET: No. Try getting really angry. Blow up.

MARCELLE: Right. *(to Paillardin, with Pinglet's boot in hand)* Aaaagh.

ANGELIQUE: Oh, my God!

PAILLARDIN: Marcelle. I beg you, don't believe everything you read. It was all a joke, I'm sure, a practical joke.

MARCELLE: Don't you dare touch me! *(inspired)* Ah, now I understand. *She* was one of your so-called ghosts.

PINGLET: That's it! For your husband it was ghosts— for my wife it was a runaway horse. And—by a strange coincidence—they slink back to their conjugal beds, both of them with a great big black eye! Where did they get them? What depraved games were they playing?

MARCELLE: Aha!

PAILLARDIN: All right. Let's stop all this. It's enough! The charges are groundless. But you believe them....

PINGLET: And how!

PAILLARDIN: So let's all of us, all four of us, go to this police inspector and see if he identifies us.

PINGLET AND MARCELLE: Ah no, no. *(they sit precisely together)*

ANGELIQUE: A very good idea. Let's go to the police station.

PINGLET AND MARCELLE: No.

PAILLARDIN: Excuse me. But yes! You've accused us. The police alone can vindicate us.

VICTOIRE: *(enters)* Monsieur Mathieu.

PINGLET AND MARCELLE: Him—oh, no.

MATHIEU: What a night. My God, what a night.

PINGLET AND MARCELLE: Oh, my God!

113

MATHIEU: Good morning, Pinglet!

PINGLET: *(taking him by the shoulders)* A good morning. How good is it? Go into my room a minute. We're very busy at the moment.

MATHIEU: Of course—good morning, Madame Paillardin. Morning, Madame Pinglet. Oh, what's the matter with your eye?

ANGELIQUE: Nothing. Nothing at all.

MATHIEU: *(Pinglet pushing, still)* If you only knew what happened to me after I left you yesterday.

PINGLET: Yes. Fine. You can tell me later.

MATHIEU: My daughters and I spent the night in a cell ...

PINGLET: ... ect hotel. Select hotel. I'm so glad. Don't pay any attention—he stutters. Terrible stutter.

MATHIEU: No, I don't. Not at all. I don't stutter.

PINGLET: Please, God. Make it rain. Make it rain.

MATHIEU: Fortunately, this morning they understood who we were, and we were given our freedom.

PINGLET: Lucky you. In there now. In we go.

MATHIEU: But I've had enough. We're going home.

PINGLET: Good! In there. *(pushes him into the bedroom)*

PAILLARDIN: What a bore.

MATHIEU: *(he re-enters)* And you two? How was the rest of the night?

PINGLET: Just fine, thank you, just fine. *(grabs him)*

MATHIEU: Watch out.

PINGLET: Go go go go.

ANGELIQUE: What did he mean by "How was the rest of the night?"

PINGLET: It's his dialect. I think he meant, "Did you have a good rest last night." In Marseilles that's how they say it.

ANGELIQUE: I didn't know that.

PAILLARDIN: Well, now for the police inspector.

MARCELLE: No, no.

VICTOIRE: *(enters)* Inspector Boucard.

MARCELLE: Oh, my God.

PAILLARDIN: The police inspector.

ANGELIQUE: Oh, good.

PINGLET: Boucard.

PAILLARDIN AND ANGELIQUE: Please come in, won't you. This way.

(Pinglet and Marcelle hide in a corner of the room)

BOUCARD: Monsieur Paillardin?

PAILLARDIN: That's me, sir.

BOUCARD: I beg your pardon, monsieur. I didn't recognize you right away. It was dark last night, and of course you were covered in soot *(pronounced suit)*!

PAILLARDIN: Soot.

BOUCARD: Suit.

PAILLARDIN: Me?

BOUCARD: But I remember you perfectly now.

PAILLARDIN AND ANGELIQUE: What ... but ...

PINGLET: —he remembers him.

PAILLARDIN: You remember me?!

BOUCARD: Perfectly ... since it was only last night I arrested you along with Madame Pinglet at the Paradise Hotel.

ANGELIQUE: You arrested me!

PAILLARDIN: Me! With her?

BOUCARD: Madame Pinglet. But of course!

ANGELIQUE: Yes, Inspector! Madame Pinglet!

BOUCARD: Excuse me, madame, it was hard to see your face last night—under the veil *(pronounced vial).*

ANGELIQUE: Veil.

BOUCARD: Vial.

ANGELIQUE: Me?

BOUCARD: But now, *(shrugs)* when you've been in the business as long as I have ... now I recognize you.

ALL: Aha. What? etc....

ANGELIQUE: You recognize *me*!

PINGLET: He does. He does. Better and better....

PAILLARDIN: Sir, it is impossible. You cannot recognize us. For the simple reason that we were never at the Paradise Hotel.

BOUCARD: Then how did I arrest you? And questioned you. And let you out on bail (bile)!

PAILLARDIN: Bail.

BOUCARD: Bile.

PAILLARDIN: It wasn't us, I tell you. It must have been a couple of people playing a practical joke.

BOUCARD: Anyway, it's of no importance now.

PAILLARDIN AND ANGELIQUE: No importance! What do you mean?

BOUCARD: I'm only sorry my secretary sent out the summonses. Now that I know who you are—it's over and done with. Monsieur Paillardin, Architect and Learned Expert to the Court in Matters of Construction and Drainage (drine-age).

PINGLET: Drainage.

PAILLARDIN: Very kind, but we needn't dwell on my qualifications. Not now. It's not relevant.

BOUCARD: Maybe not for you, but—for me it is. I've been looking for an expert in your field—for God knows how long. I didn't know who I was talking to, that's all.

PAILLARDIN: Please.

BOUCARD: And I'm really pleased I ran into you. To cut a long story short, I've got this little place in the country, and the drains ...

PAILLARDIN: I don't care about your house in the country and your drains—what about last night!

BOUCARD: Don't worry about it—you're a nice middle-class man, nice house, money in the bank, you're no problem for the police.

PAILLARDIN: Yes, but there is a problem for this lady and this gentleman.

BOUCARD: Monsieur! ... Madame! *(they bow with their backs to him)*

PAILLARDIN: Because of your summonses, our spouses believe that ... in actual fact, last night we ... er ... but since that is not true, you must make it clear that you can't identify us.

BOUCARD: I already said that!

PAILLARDIN: All right, what I mean is ... make it clear that you didn't arrest us!

BOUCARD: That's a bit more difficult.

PAILLARDIN: Think, man! Take a good look at us.

ANGELIQUE: You didn't see the lady's face, do you recall her figure, her shape ... outline?

BOUCARD: Well, now that you mention it, I think she was a little less substantial. But ... it could have been an optical illusion. After all, I've got a really big office.

PAILLARDIN: So?

BOUCARD: Might alter the scale of things a bit.

ANGELIQUE: What insolence!

BOUCARD: Only thing I remember is the dress. It was sort of a puce color.

ANGELIQUE: Is that so? There! I haven't got a puce dress.

MARCELLE: Neither have I.

PINGLET: Quiet!

PAILLARDIN: No one's talking about you.

BOUCARD: *(to Angelique)* Sorry, madame, that's the best I can do.

PAILLARDIN: We demand an official investigation.

118

BOUCARD: An investigation! ... Now about this drainage problem in the country....

PAILLARDIN: Later. Later. Now you arrested some other people last night, didn't you? Question them. See if they recognize us. Who were these people?

BOUCARD: I've got a list somewhere.... *(takes out book)*

PAILLARDIN: Let me have a look ... Gaston the Stud-no. Adele Dubois, also known as Fifi the Floozie. Bastien Bahadur, Hotel Manager, Mathieu and daughters.

ANGELIQUE: Mathieu, what Mathieu? We've got a Mathieu in the house.

BOUCARD: Here?

PINGLET: Damn!

ANGELIQUE: Yes, in there, and he has four daughters.

PAILLARDIN: He did say he spent the night in a cel—

PINGLET: —ect hotel.

PAILLARDIN: No, you said "ect," he said "cell."

BOUCARD: Must be him.

ANGELIQUE: Let's find out for sure. We'll ask him in person. Mathieu! Mathieu!

MARCELLE: I wish the ground would open up beneath me.

PINGLET: So do I.

ANGELIQUE AND PAILLARDIN: Monsieur Mathieu.

(Mathieu appears).

MATHIEU: What is it? What do you want?

PINGLET: Come on out.

MATHIEU: The police inspector! What have I done now! *(runs, but is prevented)*

PAILLARDIN: You can help us explain an impossible situation.

ANGELIQUE: Now speak the truth. I know that you can save us.

BOUCARD: Monsieur Mathieu, try now, just try to remember everything that happened.

MATHIEU: Please! Gentlemen! Madame. What do you want to ask me?

PINGLET: Why can't he stutter now?

PAILLARDIN: Last night you were, were you not, at the Paradise Hotel?

MATHIEU: Yes, I was there. I'll never forget last night. They arrested me.

(Pinglet and Marcelle try to tiptoe out)

PAILLARDIN: No one cares about that now. Tell me, did you see me and Madame Pinglet there?

MATHIEU: No. I didn't see you.

ANGELIQUE AND PAILLARDIN: There! Do you hear that?

MATHIEU: When I think of my little girls! Locked up, weeping, shivering, thrown into the cells ...

PAILLARDIN: No one cares about that. But if you didn't see us, who did you see?

MATHIEU: Well, in fact I saw ... my poor little daughters.

PAILLARDIN: I told you no one cares about that.

ANGELIQUE: Who did you see?

MATHIEU: I can tell you right now.

PINGLET: It's all over.

MATHIEU: Pinglet! Isn't this a riot? They're asking me who I saw.

PINGLET: *(laughing)* I know, I know.

MATHIEU: You want to know who I saw ... *(Pinglet tugs his coat)* What are you doing? Leave my coat alone. *(to Angelique)* Well, guess who I saw.... *(thunderclap, pouring rain)* As large as li-li-li ...

(Pinglet runs to window)

ANGELIQUE: What's the matter with him now?

MARCELLE: He's stuttering.

PINGLET: *(on a chair, arms raised)* Thank you, Lord. Thank you for the Blessed Rain.

MATHIEU: I sa ... s ... s ...

BOUCARD: Come on, man, spit it out.

MATHIEU: The Pa-pa-pa-pa ...

ANGELIQUE: His father was there?

MATHIEU: Ra-ra-ra ... dise ...

PINGLET: He's stuttering, really well.

MATHIEU: Ho-ho-ho ...

ANGELIQUE: It's not funny. Tell us who was there.

MATHIEU: *(indicates Marcelle)* Ma-ma-ma ...

ANGELIQUE: His mother?

PINGLET: We're getting nowhere.

BOUCARD: I've got an idea!
(all react)

BOUCARD: Yes. He's going to have to write down the names!

PAILLARDIN AND ANGELIQUE: Yes. Excellent idea ... etc. . . .

PINGLET: Damnation!

BOUCARD: Now, sit down there and write down who you saw. *(gets pen and paper)*

(Maxime enters)

MAXIME: Oh, God, it's the man from last night! *(hat over eyes)* If he recognizes me it's all over. *(puts Pinglet's black rag over his face, then puts hat on, then climbs out)*

MATHIEU: I sa ... sa ... w s ...

PINGLET AND MARCELLE: This is it.

ANGELIQUE AND BOUCARD AND PAILLARDIN: Write it down!

MATHIEU: Pi ... Pi ... Pi ...

PINGLET: Stop, thief!

ALL: Hubbub. *(Pinglet grabs Maxime)*

BOUCARD: *(to Pinglet)* Excuse me, sir, that's my job. I arrest you in the name of the law.

MAXIME: Let me go.

BOUCARD: Take off that disguise.

MAXIME: No, no. *(he takes off the handkerchief which has now covered his face with soot)*

ALL: Maxime!

BOUCARD: Aha, the man from last night!

ALL: What?

BOUCARD: The man who was covered in suit.

ALL: Soot.

BOUCARD: Look! There he is.

PAILLARDIN: Maxime, you young devil you. Was it you?

MAXIME: Was what me? What are you all talking about?

BOUCARD: Did you or did you not spend last night at the Paradise Hotel?

MAXIME: How did you know?

ALL: It was him.

PINGLET: He confessed. He confessed.

MATHIEU: But the fact is, *(thunder)* I—I—

PINGLET: Shut up! *(hits him)*

ANGELIQUE: And with whom did you spend the night. You dare not say that it was with me!

MAXIME: With you? My God, no!

BOUCARD: Then with whom? Because you were with a woman.

ALL: With whom?

MAXIME: Oh, all right. I give up. With Victoire.

ALL: Victoire!

PAILLARDIN: Where is she. Where is this Victoire?

ANGELIQUE: In her room.

PAILLARDIN: In her room. Just a minute. Victoire! Victoire!

MATHIEU: Yes, but it wa-was ...

PINGLET: I told you to shut up. *(hits him)*

MATHIEU: All rig-right. *(he's writing)*

PAILLARDIN: Come on, come down.

VICTOIRE: Just a minute.

PAILLARDIN: Come out here, girl....

ALL: The puce dress!

ANGELIQUE: Where did you get the dress?

VICTOIRE: I was just trying it on! Someone gave it to me and ...

PINGLET: Oh, there's no need for long explanations.

PAILLARDIN: Last night, were you at the Paradise Hotel?

VICTOIRE: How did you know?!

ANGELIQUE: And you had the audacity to pretend you were me?

VICTOIRE: What? But ...

PINGLET: I said there's no need for long explanations. Just get out. Get out of our house. Pack your things.

ANGELIQUE: Just a minute, Pinglet.

PINGLET: I've heard quite enough from you, too. *(to Victoire)* I told you, pack your things. Never darken my door again. *(aside to her)* I'll talk to you later.

VICTOIRE: *(exiting)* They're crazy. Completely crazy.

PINGLET: Now then ...

MATHIEU: Here's my sta-stat ...

PINGLET: Statement? Well, we don't need that now, do we? We know what happened.

ALL: No. We know what happened. We don't need it now.

(Pinglet tears it up)

MATHIEU: Oh.

PINGLET: It's time for your train. If you don't hurry you'll miss it. Back to Marseilles.

(all push Mathieu to door)

ALL: Back to Marseilles.

MATHIEU: Bu-bu-bu its po-po-pouring rain.

PINGLET: *(shuts his mouth)* It'll be fine in Marseilles. *(out he goes)*

PINGLET: Pouf. Thank God.

BOUCARD: Well, young man, I trust that this is the last we'll hear of this little episode. Allow me to return your five thousand francs.

MAXIME: My five thousand francs.

PINGLET: What's he doing, that's mine!

MAXIME: How do they belong to me?

BOUCARD: Because you were the man at the Paradise Hotel.

MAXIME: And they give you a rebate?

PINGLET: He gets everything and I get nothing.

MAXIME: It's a very good hotel. I'm going back there.

PINGLET: Well, I'm never going back. Never! Never!! *(seeing Marcelle and changing his tone)* Never.

ELEPHANT PAPERBACKS